Exhibition Dates

Rice Museum, Houston
April 14 to June 11, 1978

LEGER
Our Contemporary

INSTITUTE FOR THE ARTS, RICE UNIVERSITY, 1978.

Acknowledgments

This exhibition was made possible by the generous loans of paintings and drawings in Texas collections or which were previously in Texas. Though far from being comprehensive, the selection gives a spectrum of Léger's work, ranging from a drawing of 1912 to a painting of 1954. It includes material never published before, in particular three sketches for a mural that is now destroyed.

We are immensely grateful to the lenders for sharing their treasures, and we wish to express to them our deepest thanks on behalf of the public, which will have a rare chance of appreciating anew Léger's scope.

D.M.

Lenders

Sarah Campbell Blaffer Foundation at the University of Houston
    Blaffer Gallery
Mr. and Mrs. James H. Clark, Dallas
Mr. and Mrs. Charles V. Hooks, Houston
Jeffrey Horvitz Ltd., Los Angeles
Katherine and Benjamin Kitchen, Houston
Janie C. Lee Gallery, Houston
The Sylvan and Mary Lang Collection, McNay Art Institute,
    San Antonio
Menil Foundation Collection, Houston
Lois and George de Menil, Paris
The Museum of Fine Arts, Houston
Five anonymous lenders

Léger, Our Contemporary

Fernand Léger died in 1955. More than twenty years later and thousands of miles away, he appears strangely close, strangely in tune with the beat of young cities, born on the prairie and budding with buildings.

Maybe his vigorous and epic style can be appreciated more easily in Dallas or Houston than in sophisticated centers of culture. There is a naïveté, a directness and a fundamental optimism in Léger's art that is akin to the naïveté, directness and optimism of a frontiersman. In him no nostalgia for the past, no multiple layers of reading. Everything stated is frontal, straightforward and colorful.

The discovery of Cézanne was the greatest event in Léger's life as an artist. Through Cézanne's influence he developed his own brand of Cubism, which owed nothing to Picasso or Braque. For years he kept looking at Cézanne: "I was never finished exploring and discovering. Cézanne taught me the love of forms and volumes."[1]

Besides Cézanne, Léger acknowledged only the Romanesque and Byzantine artists. Overlooking centuries of artistic creativity he could say with total sincerity: "Between Giotto and us (the modern painters) I see nothing."[2] Like the Byzantine artists, he tended to transcend naturalism, to reach out for heroic dimensions. His taste was for the formal, the severe, the hieratic. This inclination must have had deep psychological roots in the cultural history of France, in its tradition of measure and restraint. At heart he was French and classical: "Je suis un classique," he used to say. Indeed he was. There is not a trace of romanticism in his work, nothing erotic or morbid, nothing subjective, not a shadow of sentimentality. For all his audacity and modernity, he remained traditional in his approach to art and in his craft. He never departed from the most conventional means, never introduced collage into his paintings, never dabbled in "mixed mediums." To him all problems were plastic ones, and oil, gouache, ink and pencil were all he needed to solve them.

Everywhere Léger found plastic beauty. Everything he drew acquired dignity and monumentality, be it a screw, a twisted wire or just a rag. Every person became majestic, fit to decorate the pediments of some modern temple.

Alas, our time provided no Pericles and there was no community capable of truly understanding the heroic dimension of his art.

Yet, he seized each opportunity offered to him to work on an architectural scale. He dreamt of great murals celebrating the labor and leisure of workers. To the end he kept the illusion that his painting would be appreciated by the workers themselves, "les camarades, les gas." He felt close to them, one of them. But the workers were impervious to his art. They preferred the "chromos" hanging on their walls which raised no problem. Exhausted by a day's work they cared only for sports news and Edith Piaf.

Perhaps the closest Léger ever came to being appreciated by workers was when the opportunity was given to him in 1950 to decorate a newly built church in an industrial neighborhood. The series of monumental stained glass windows he did at Audincourt, in the vicinity of Peugeot factories, found understanding and love from the workers who were themselves contributing manual labor to their church. Those windows may well be his masterpiece.

Léger's prodigious gifts became only slowly recognized. Yet he dominates the artistic scene of his time. His deep originality appears today as the purest expression of the French classical tradition.

Dominique de Menil, Director
Institute for the Arts, Rice University

1. "Je n'en finissais pas d'explorer et de découvrir. Cézanne m'a appris l'amour des formes et des volumes. . . ." *Fernand Léger 1881-1955* (Musée des Arts Décoratifs — Palais du Louvre, 1956), p. 76.
2. "Entre Giotto et nous, je ne vois rien. . . ." *L'Art Sacré* (July-August, 1950), p. 25.

LEGER NOW
Amy Goldin

Who are our contemporaries? The question is fundamentally a political one. Our social environment includes bodies in all stages of historical development: fetuses, disintegrating .debris, inert material — and our contemporaries, those who stand in more or less the same relationship to the world that we do. To name one's contemporaries is to decide what issues and involvements seem to us immediate and urgent. Our contemporaries are those who address themselves to whatever we experience as our present condition.

I wish to claim Léger as a contemporary, and I don't think that discussions of art history, Cubism, influences, etc. can offer anything in substantiation of that claim. Practically speaking, both the future and the past are constructed out of the present moment. The first question is "Where are we?" All the rest is literature.

For me, Léger was a piece of art history for a very long time. Being a respectful sort by nature, I was dutifully and distastefully looking at *Big Julie* one afternoon at the Museum of Modern Art when it suddenly struck me that the butterfly alone weighs a good five pounds. This amused me; I smiled; Big Julie remained glum. I saw the goddess as a dumb broad, and Léger became my contemporary. Or, more precisely, I became his. Because Léger, with his disinterest in expression and fluidity, his hardheaded contempt for charm and fingertip sensuality, had been way ahead of me.

There are other people I know who switched on to Léger in the same abrupt way after a long period of accepting him as part of museum furnishings. We were all misled, I think, by the very grounds on which his modernity had been offered, by his preoccupation with the machine. Yet it is in those pictures where Léger is most blatantly involved with the romance of the machine that he now looks most dated (which is not to say that those paintings are artistically his least successful). What is contemporary in Léger is his psychological detachment — the "inexpressiveness" — and his complementary engagement with the physical. We can recognize both of these attitudes as our own. What is less familiar to us is Léger's progressive detachment from technology, and here, I believe, he precedes us, because a lot of artists are still hung up on technology as a way of being modern. But what is involved in being modern? Objectively speaking, there is no reason why an automated factory cannot be built to produce plastic horse-collars — which is to say that the most advanced methods and materials can be used to turn out a product that is itself anachronistic. Indeed, such lapses in contemporary relevance are all too common, both inside and outside the modern art world.

However, the relevance of physicality to contemporary art is a proposition that needs careful explaining if it is not to remain uselessly vague. In the context of Léger's work it has nothing to do with materials or the ultimately physical nature of the art object. It has nothing to do with machines, but it does have something — not much — to do with subject matter. Subject matter is at best a crude indication of an artist's interests, and in Léger's case it would be easy to conclude too much from his iconographic palette of women, workers, plants and domestic objects. Despite his old-left politics, I don't think Léger painted the things he did because he wanted to "say" anything about them, but because he liked them. Their value was simply that he found them real, authentic, and for him that was the same thing as being heroic. Strictly speaking, his clouds and tin cans, hand-painted ties and the Mona Lisa were all real, all equally noble and equally ignoble. This is a violently democratic idea, but certainly not a common or popular one. Léger himself insisted that he approached *all* his subjects as objects. When someone pointed out that the smiling circus artists in the *Big Parade* were violating his "no expression" canon, he protested. "For performers," he said, "a smile is not an expression, it's part of the job."

Léger saw the painter's job, his *métier*, in secular but traditional terms. The artist makes pictures of life, and life is whatever is truly modern and real. But "modern" and "real" are not categories but qualifiers. Léger's words don't tell us much. To find out what he meant we must go to the work. He was always a figurative artist, even when the "figures" are completely abstract. His forms are always articulated in relation to a ground. In the late work they are even more regularly referential than they were during the early periods.

Yet it is a peculiar relationship to subject matter that ends up treating all subjects impartially, and a peculiar sort of reality that sounds a single emotional note regardless of what is painted.

Mondrian, with his various rhythms, is less monotonous in feeling than Léger. In their own way, Léger's productions are as abstract and formalized as soap opera. He himself seemed unaware of his abstractness. His expectations of his "new realism" were touchingly naïve. When the *Construction Workers* was finished Léger had it mounted on the wall of the canteen in the Renault factory and sat anonymously at a table waiting for the workers' response. When the men laughed and said that nobody could work with hands like that he was disappointed. So much for the myth of Léger, robust son of a robust people.

Yet we stubbornly feel that somehow the myth is true. Compared to Picasso, Braque, and Matisse, Léger is not an also-ran, but somehow more radically "modern" than they, and uniquely close to "reality." The grounds for this feeling must lie in the work, more particularly in its use of form.

For Léger, the ineradicable core of reality and objecthood was, quite simply, massiveness. Spiritual presence or emotional impact is interpreted, with startling directness, as physical density and volume. Thus the leaves that look like hamburgers, the plasticene clouds, the smoke rings as palpable as balloons. "Life is hard and heavy," said Léger.

Which is how he painted it. For him, reality was not an objective, quasi-scientific phenomenon, but the pressure of experience. All sensations have the impact of weight. But once we have seen the force, the obviousness and the downright banality of his central metaphor, the work of criticism remains to be done. Because, after all, how did he manage it? A direct visceral appeal somehow transforms having a body into something the spectator *shares* with the image, so that seeing the picture creates a situation that entails and bestows solidity, an immediate experience of endurance and energy.

Moreover, oddly central to the physicality of this art is its humorousness. There is definitely something comical in Léger, something dopey, a highly physical, utterly non-verbal *wit*, totally unlike the boulevardier humor of Klee or Grosz, with its overtones of the gallows. It is closer to the sexual humor of Miro or Oldenburg, but deeper, at once more physical and more abstract than that. You can see the same sort of thing in the choreography of Yvonne Rainer. As if there were something comical about having a body altogether. Or as if some sort of exuberance pops up when physical energy is freed from psychological conditions. Léger's forms strike us as holding up under pressure — is it the hidden assurance of the indestructibility of the body that delights us?

Having come to no conclusions about that, I want to let it lie there. and return to the surer ground of Léger's pictorial form. There are artistic difficulties implicit in Léger's insistence on the presence of volume since it does not allow the same sort of pictorial construction that elsewhere grew out of Cubism. Pictorial volume directly threatens the integrity of the picture plane, and in general modern art has tended to preserve the plane above all. The business of making pictures is interpreted as a matter of energizing the surface without breaking it or getting visibly fussy, and plasticity has been reassigned to sculpture and architecture. Artistic energy itself is seen as leaning on the insitition of movement rather than mass. Moreover, in modern art, movement is understood to be a linear force, not an expansive one. Movement in our time is directional thrust, expressed either as painterly gesture or as the axis of primary or sequential forms in sculpture. The artistic experience of mass has all but disappeared. In exchange we are offered gigantic size, an eviscerated monumentality that corresponds to the contemporary idea of power.

In classical Western painting, the problem of distributing mass throughout the picture became the problem of balance, and the "logical" distribution of weight required every pictorial element to be supported by another, so that everything balanced out and rested ultimately on the ground plane. The force of gravity was always visible, and the architecture of pictorial forms was seen as a strict analogue of the architecture of real weight and mass. Modern art has dispensed with all that, throwing the idea of pictorial structure up for grabs. We no longer know what it is, except that it seems to have something to do with the picture plane.

Léger, however, was French enough to assume that the classical principles of pictorial structure were eternal. Consequently he proceeded to solve a very modern problem — reconciling the distribution of visual mass with the design requirements of the picture plane — in a thoroughly straightforward and satisfactory way. Indications of mass and plane are interlaced and amalgamated, always in a strict parallel to the picture plane, in such a way as to give every pictorial development (across the surface or into space) its counter-indication. Tying everything together is an outline that alternates between being the edge of a flat shape and the contour of a form, with a few side excursions into pure arabesque or pattern.

If we compare the study and the final version of the 1930 *Composition with a Top* we have a remarkably clear demonstration of the sources of Léger's artistic power, because the two are so very close and the final version is so very much the better picture. Our first impression is that the final version is more spacious and less crowded than the study. In fact there is a small difference in the proportions of the two formats. The large canvas is slightly narrower, but has a pervasive sense of increased breadth and looseness. All of Léger's modifications here serve to counteract the vertical gravitational pull of the study without lightening the massiveness of the component forms. In both versions the heaviest element is the tall black silhouette just left of center. The major changes are those which modify the weight of this form. Taking out the line in the white below it strengthened the hook-shape so that it came forward to cradle and contain the black, and stepping the bottom left contour of the black form sets the top into a clearly foremost and dominant position.

Most of Léger's usual construction devices are clearly visible here: the alternation of straight line and curve, the reversals of position among overlapping forms, a single color appearing now in front, now behind. The palette is very limited, keyed to the intensity of black and white. Léger avoids vibrancy — complementaries are rarely jux-taposed — and if the colors were not constantly shifting position, moving ahead and behind, they would be monotonous. See how much the mobility of the big yellow shape at the right is increased by the little white footprint that has been slipped behind its right edge. Freed from an unbroken supporting plane, the yellow begins to ripple like its white counterpart on the left.

All this back-and-forth business is going on at right angles to the surface — a third dimensional dynamic that does not disturb the lateral stability of the image. That is still locked to the format and the picture plane by the repetition of horizontals and verticals parallel to the edges of the canvas. Léger seems to spend half his time building protective frames around his forms (the head encircled by an arm is a very characteristic gesture) and half the time slamming a new color or shape in front of them. The middle of the picture plane acts as a center of energy, countervailing the force of gravity and drawing the major shapes around it while secondary and small-scale forms tend to break

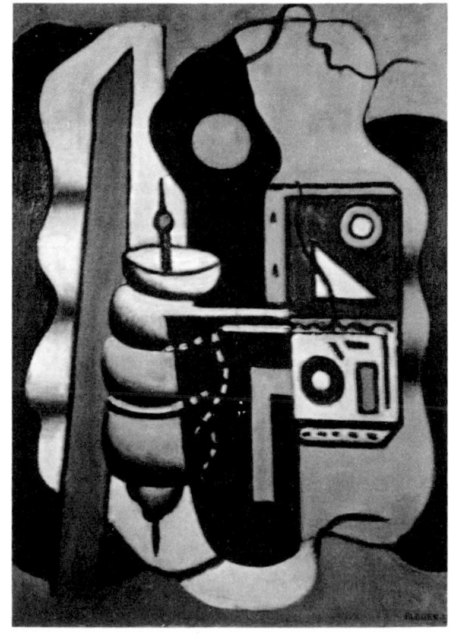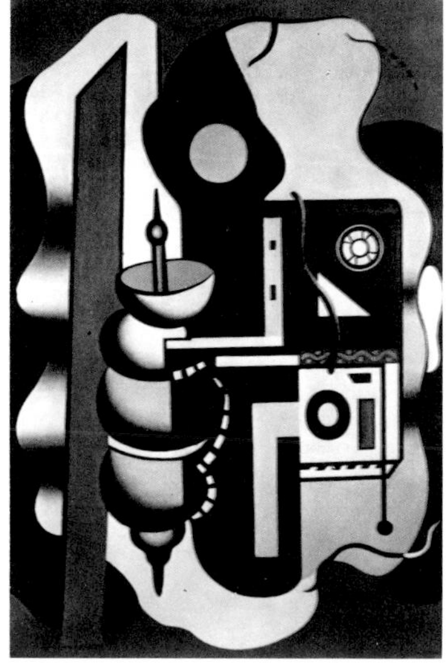

Léger's sketch (left) *Composition with a Top*, 1929, 25⅝ x 18⅛ inches, and his final version (right), 1930, 57½ x 38¼ inches. (Not in the exhibition; photos courtesy of Perls Gallery, New York.)

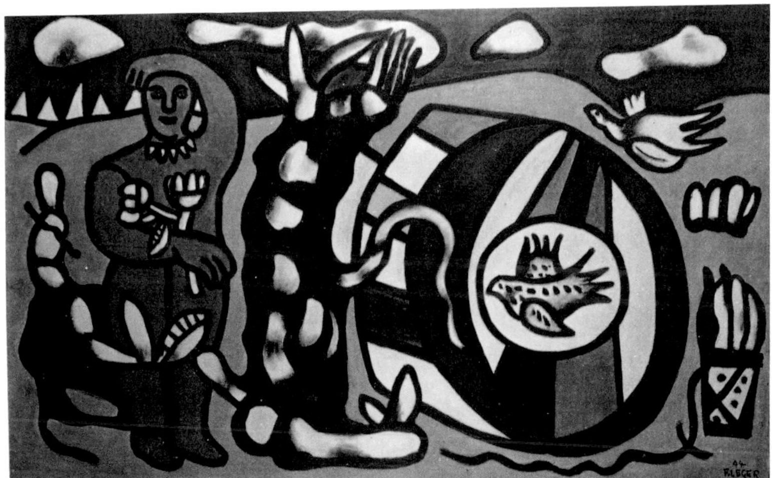

The Young Indian Woman, 1944, 32 x 51¼ inches. (Not in the exhibition; photo courtesy of Perls Gallery, New York.)

away. When the complex forces at work are insufficiently articulated and separated the scheme doesn't come off. A nasty clot of suspended fragments, like a bunch of octopuses locked in a death-struggle, seems to be floating by.

Around 1940 Léger began to experiment with new ways of opening up pictorial space. *The Construction Workers* and some of the late still-lifes use a centrifugal composition, with the forms dispersing outward from a central vertical axis. Even earlier Léger had at times dropped local color and tried to set up a fugue-like situation in which the line establishes one series of forms, color areas another. He kept trying to make this idea work until the end of his life. But Léger neither was nor wanted to be a facile artist, and a control of color came especially hard to him. He couldn't put down a veil of anything — his palest yellow lies on the surface like a rug. Even if the brilliance of the white were not annihilated by the thick black lines of drawing it could not support the density of his colors. Since the color and line don't reinforce each other, and since neither creates a satisfactory plastic situation in itself, these paintings end up by being structureless. Everything goes flat and dull — the wandering streams of black muddy the color without interrupting it.

On the other hand, when Léger dispensed with the white ground, his color became capable of playing a more powerful role than it ever had before. *The Young Indian* of 1944 is a beautifully realized painting, taut, brilliant, expansive and full of Léger's mysterious teasing humor. Here the articulation of space and form owes nothing to Cubism and almost everything to color. Everything is weighty, yet wholly sustained — you could float a battleship on that orange. How firmly but lightly the red Indian is poised within it! Notice the play between the real bird and the painted bird on the drum. Despite the modeling on the painted bird it stays flat within its plane, while the real bird is solid and free, held up by the strong colors that surround it. The antigravity factors in this painting are completely effective — all the most active forms point straight up while those directed downward decline slowly and obliquely. Here, too, Léger seems in unusually full control of his decorative elements. There is not the sudden shift in scale for details that for me often mars the earlier work.

Nowhere does Léger express any intention of making structural or formal innovations in art. His idea of the painter's *métier* was, as I said, traditional, and his excursions into film, mural painting and sculpture were not formally radical either. Léger is modern innocently and nonanalytically, by temperament, like Andy Warhol. And, like Warhol, the esthetic conventions he placidly accepts are as integral to his modern style as the violations of convention he instinctively introduces.

In stressing Léger's artistic emphasis on weight and physicality we face the challenge of justifying these things as values. The physical has never been considered an independent source of value — though indeed it has some history as a diabolic force, antithetical to spirit. There is no question of turning Léger into an advocate of physical fitness or some neo-Greek ideal of physical harmony. He has nothing to do with muscle-building. The importance of physicality in contemporary art lies in its implied insistence on the primacy of direct experience. Physicality emphasizes experience, not information, as the basis of human response. Information is symbolic, precise and decipherable. Experience is direct, physical and existential. For all of us, identity must begin in the body and be nourished by the senses if it is to sustain the onslaught of modern technology. Moreover, our bodies have a unique and crucial relationship to history. In our bodies it is always here and now. Yet our bodies learn, they incorporate the past and carry it into the present in the form of scars and developed sensitivities.

Being clever seems to have left us so disoriented and confused that it might be sobering to connect with being just bodies for a while. This is what Léger gives us: the feeling of a purely physical existence. And it is a "feeling" more than a vision, because these paintings insist on plasticity: sensations of mass, fullness and tautness. Léger's bodies are specifically limited and located. At his best we experience firmness without rigidity, the kind of sexless, direct energy that elsewhere in our society is celebrated as a spiritual ideal. In gesture, Léger's plants are more violent than his people, but for Léger everything is a body and bodies aren't deathly, they don't commit suicide or murder. Art that stresses the physical aspect of existence presently seems hygienic to us, and the more visceral our response, the more likely we are to call art good. Which is why Léger is so satisfying now.

Always, because of the density of his forms, Léger runs the risk of clumsiness. He is always threatened by bloat and the muscle-bound cloddishness of a hung-over Mr. Clean. It's easy to fault Léger when he's bad, but it's a lot harder to account for his quality when he's good.

What can you say of those ladies drinking tea, female deities as beautiful as cows? Léger's sensuality is so profound that Michelangelo seems petty: "He couldn't paint an arm without thinking about muscles!" So violent a celebrant of life that when he was asked for his ideas of how to decorate the city of Paris for a fête he wanted to paint the avenues different colors, all the façades on one boulevard yellow, on another blue, ". . . and Notre Dame in tricolor." Such a scheme, he explained in perfect seriousness, would help to guide tourists around the streets, and it could look great at night if you had helicopters overhead shooting down beams of light.

It would have been nice to see André Malraux's reaction to that!

CATALOGUE

All measurements are given first in inches, and then in centimeters parenthetically, in the order of height, then width.

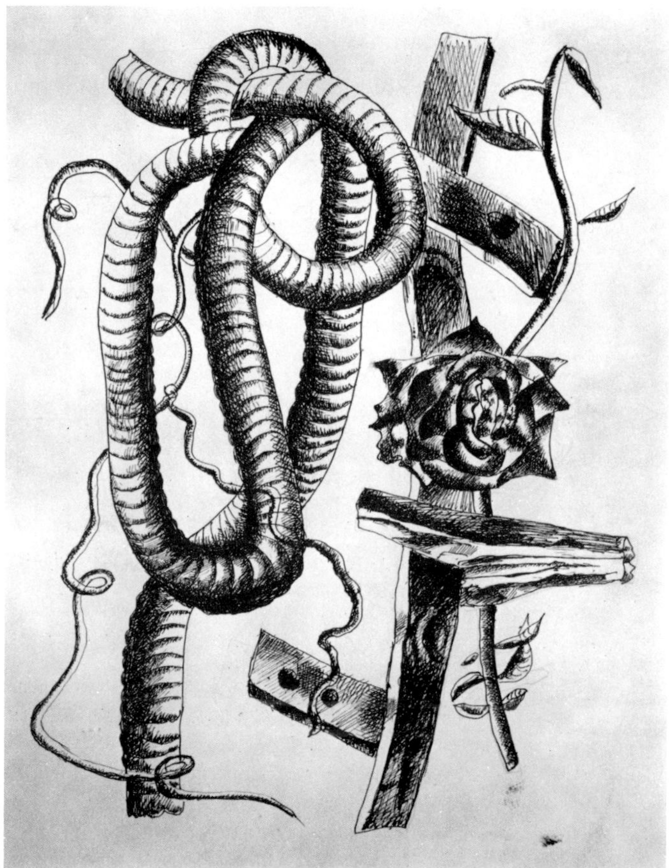

1. *Still Life with Rose and Rope.* n.d. Pen and ink on paper. 14⅛ x 10⅝ (35.9 x 27). F L, verso. (The only undated work in the catalogue, this drawing is placed outside the chronological order.)

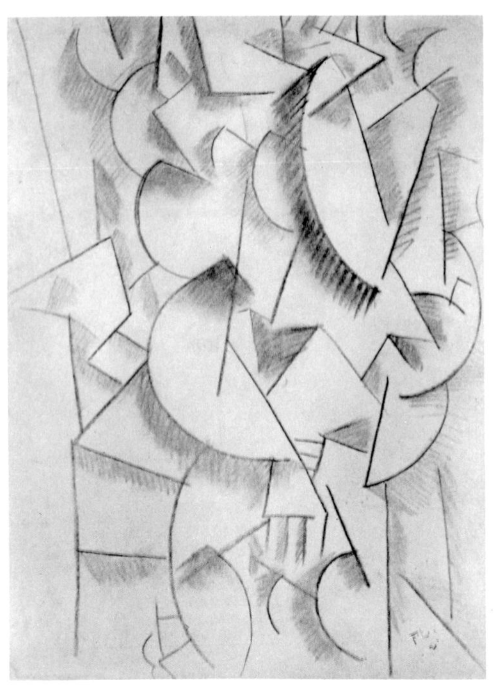

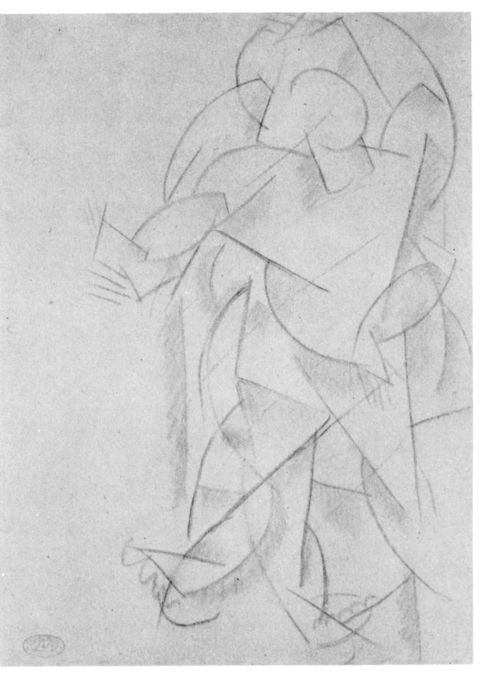

2. *Form Variations.* 1912. Recto-verso drawings, pencil on paper. 25 x 18⅛ (63.5 x 46). F. L./12, lower right recto; *Variations de form*, possibly in another hand, top center verso; and Galerie Kahnweiler stamp numbered *1814*, lower left verso.

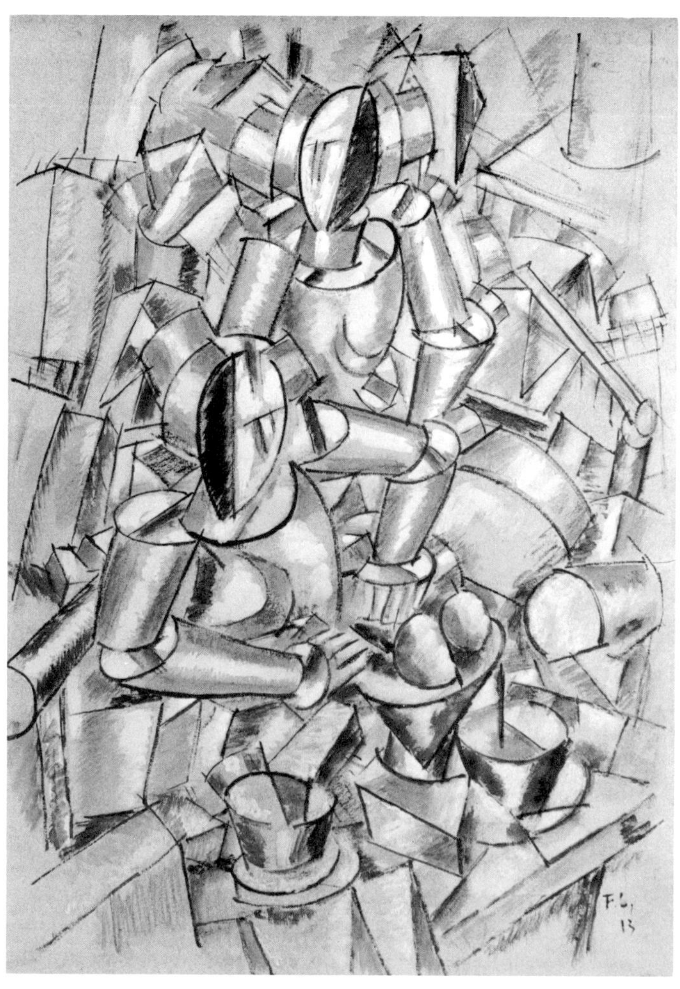

3. *Deux femmes, l'une attablée (Two Women, One at Table).*
1913. Gouache on paper. 21½ x 14¾ (54.6 x 37.5). F. L, 13,
lower right.

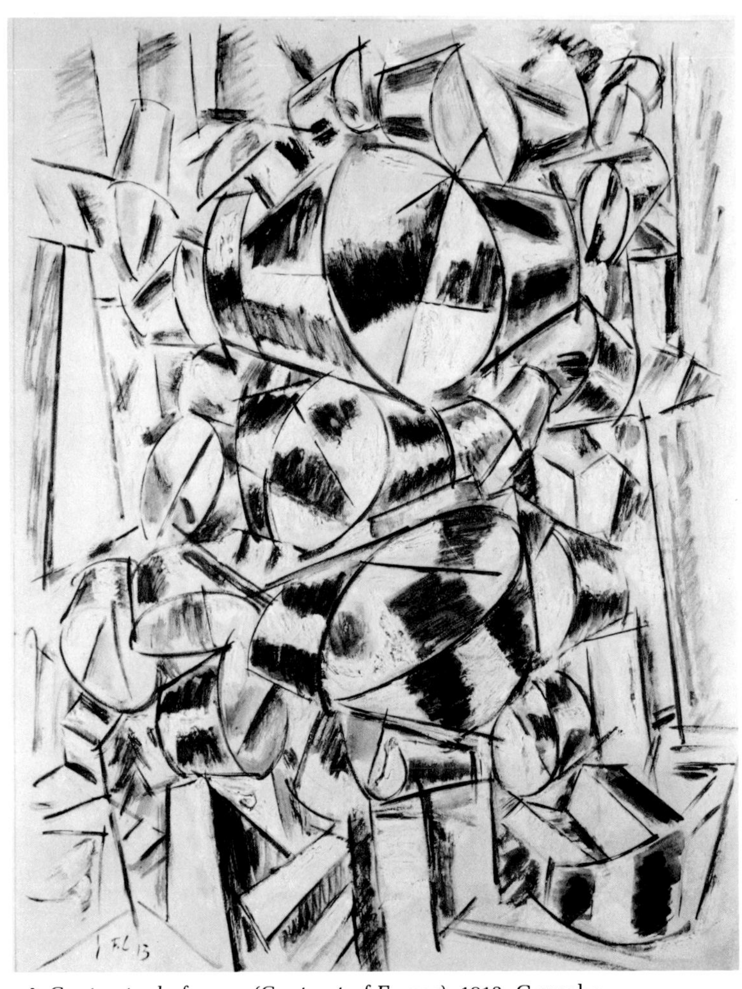

4. *Contraste de formes (Contrast of Forms)*. 1913. Gouache
on paper. 19¾ x 14½ (50.2 x 36.9). *F. L 13*, lower left.

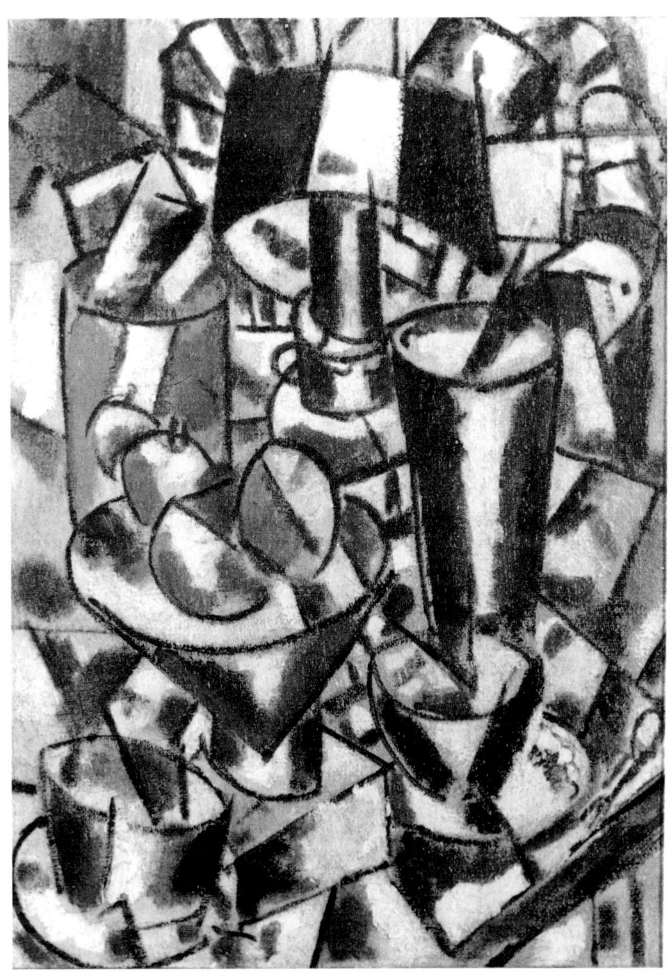

5. *Nature morte à la lampe (Still Life with Lamp)*. 1914. Oil
on canvas. 25½ x 18 (64.8 x 45.7). *F. Leger 1914*, on back. Mr
and Mrs. James H. Clark, Dallas.

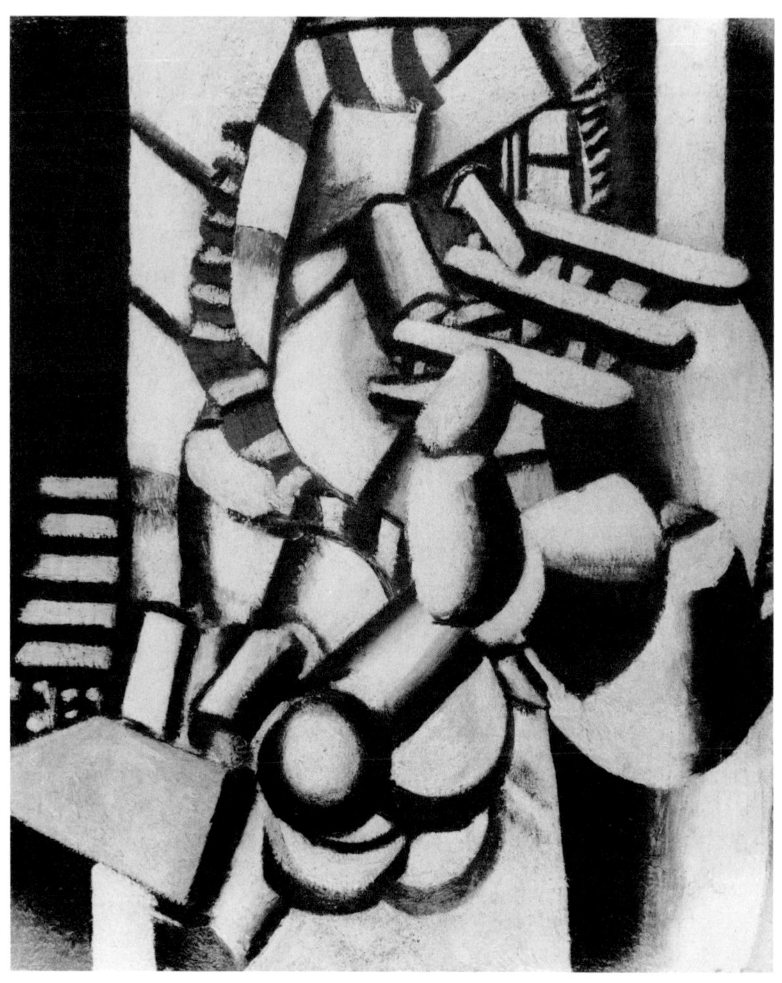

6. *Le Blessé (The Wounded).* 1918. Oil on canvas. 24 x 18⅛ (61 x 46). *F LEGER,* lower right; *Painted in 1918 Fernand Léger,* on back.

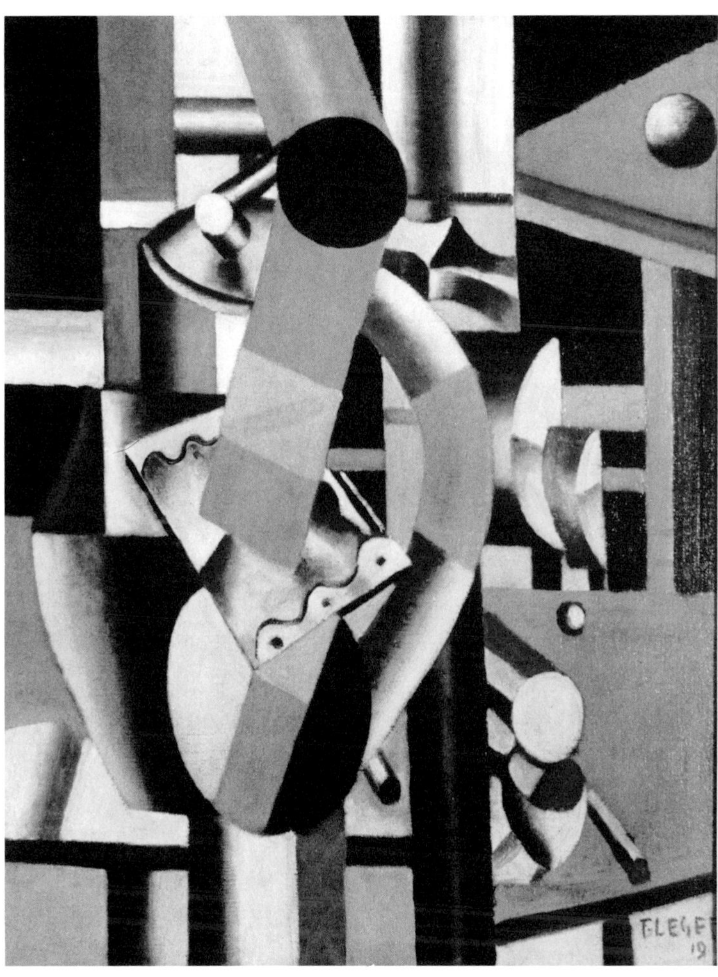

7. *Mechanical Forms.* 1919. Oil on canvas. 25½ x 19½ (64.8 x 49.5). *F. LEGER/19,* lower right. Mr. and Mrs. James H. Clark, Dallas.

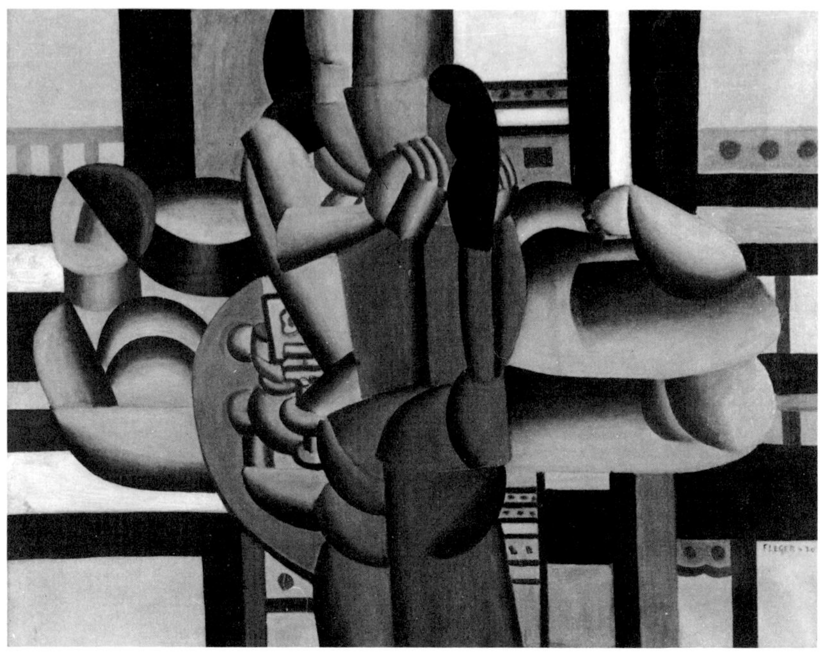

8. *Les trois Femmes et la nature morte (Three Women and Still Life).* 1920. Oil on canvas. 28¾ x 36 (73 x 91.4). F. LEGER – 20, lower right. Mr. and Mrs. James H. Clark, Dallas.

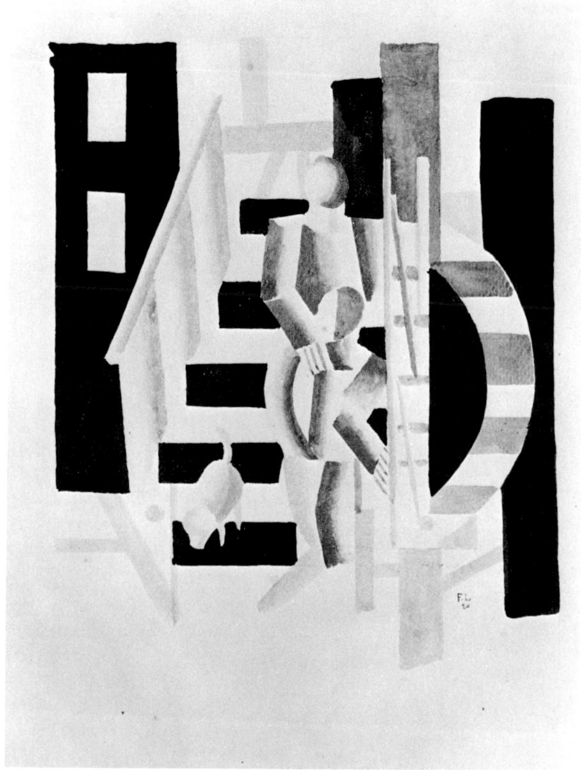

9. *Deux personnages avec chien dans un escalier (Two Figures with Dog on Stairs).* 1920. Ink wash on paper. 11 x 8½ (28 x 21.6). *F. L./20,* lower right. Menil Foundation Collection, Houston.

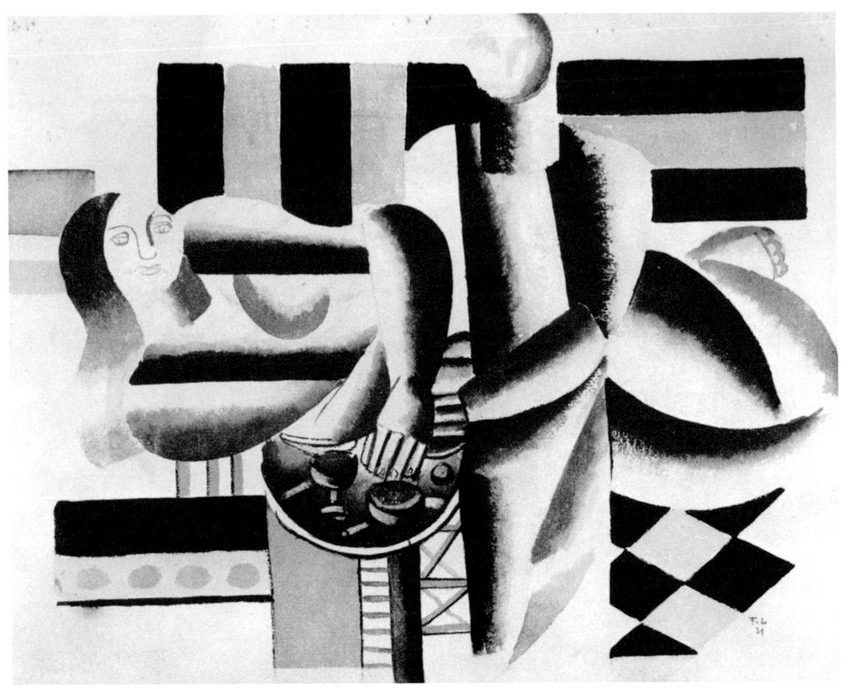

10. *Study for "The Three Women."* 1921. Watercolor on paper. 9½ x 12¼ (24.1 x 31). F. L/21, lower right. The Museum of Fine Arts, Houston, Gift of Madame Helena Rubenstein.

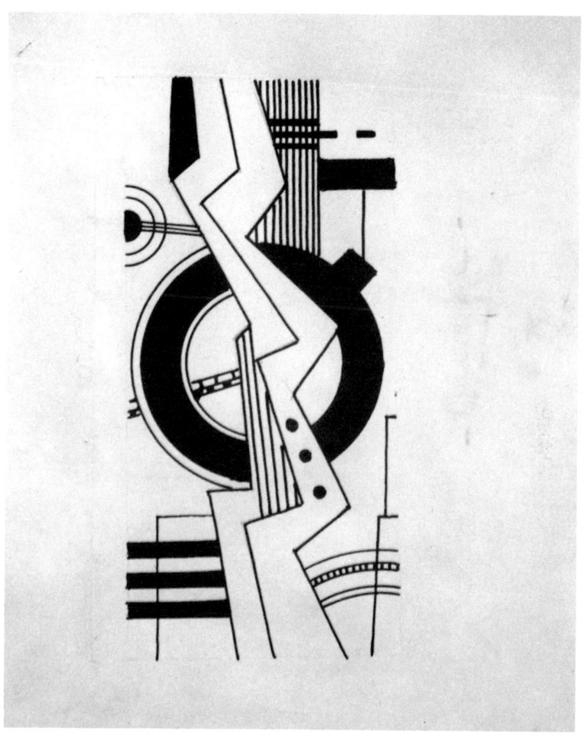

11. *Composition géométrique (Geometric Composition).* c. 1924. Pen and ink on paper. 10⅝ x 8¼ (27 x 21). Unsigned.

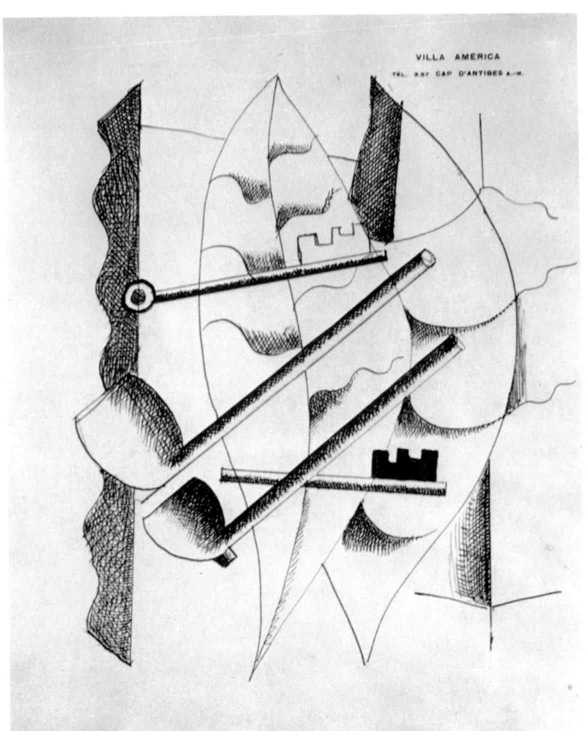

12. *Composition aux pipes (Composition with Pipes).* c. 1924. Pen and ink on Villa America stationery. 10¼ x 8¼ (26 x 21). Unsigned. *This drawing must have been made during one of Léger's stays at Gerald Murphy's house in Antibes, the Villa America.*

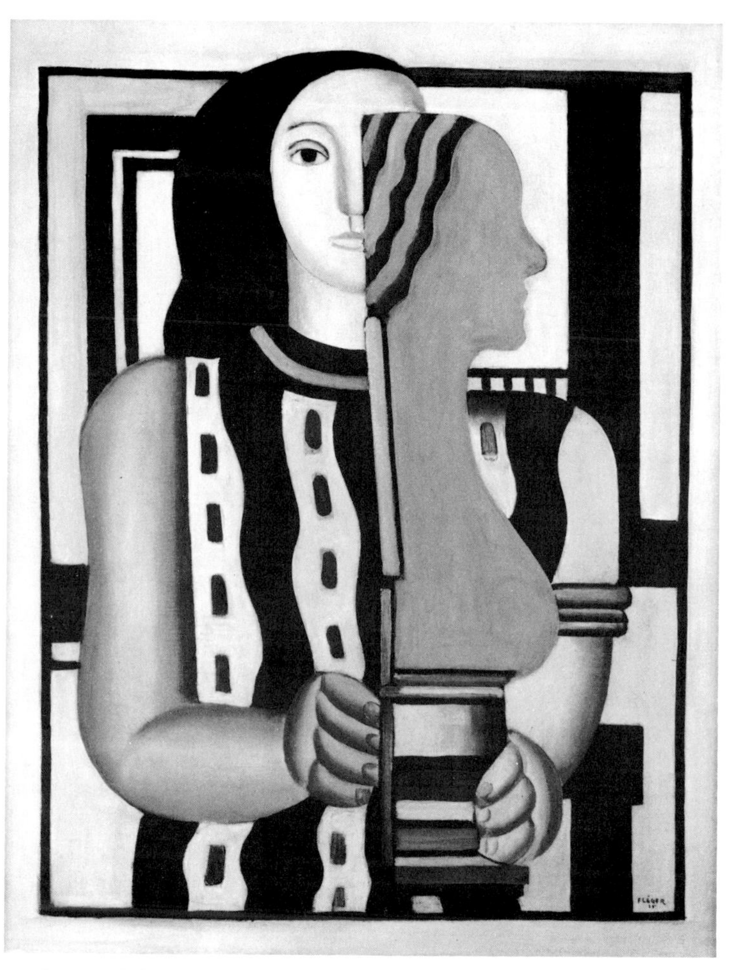

13. *Femme à la statue (Woman with Statue).* 1925. Oil on canvas. 25⅝ x 20 (65.1 x 50.8). *F LÉGER /25,* lower right. Katherine and Benjamin Kitchen, Houston.

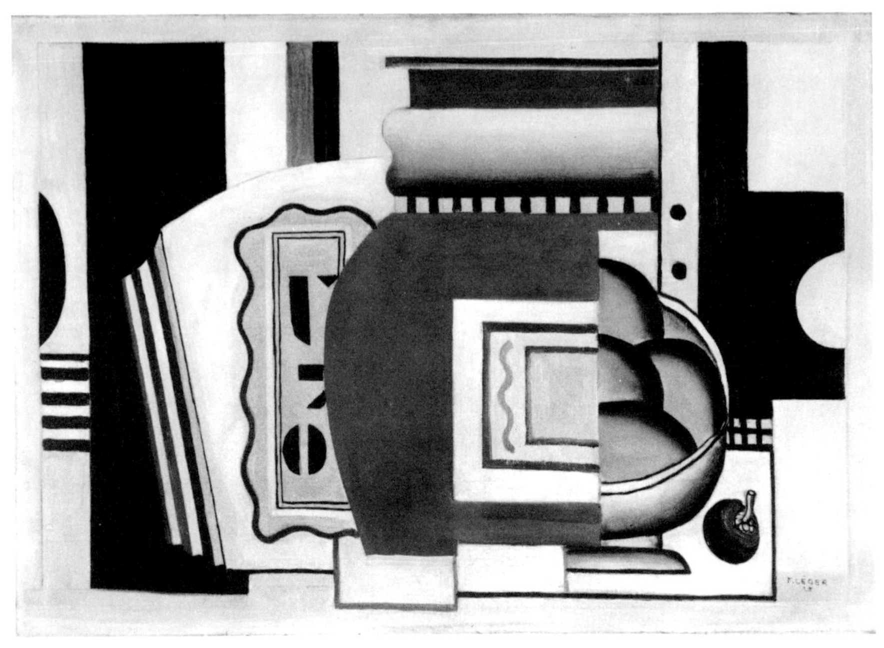

14. *Nature morte, premier état (Still Life, first state).* 1925. Oil on canvas. 18¼ x 25¾ (46.4 x 65.4). *F. LÉGER /25,* lower right; *nature-morte /1er ETAT. /F. LÉGER /25,* on back (now hidden by relining).

15. *Peinture murale (Mural Painting).* 1926. Oil on canvas. 70⅞ x 31½ (180 x 80). *F. LÉGER /26,* lower right. Menil Foundation Collection, Houston. *One of several paintings done from 1924 to 1926 which Léger conceived in the same severe, entirely abstract style under the combined influences of Le Corbusier and of the De Stijl exhibition at Léonce Rosenberg's. Contacts Léger had in 1923 and 1924 with the German and Russian avant-garde were also influential. They culminated in the 1925 Exposition Internationale des Arts Décoratifs in Paris, where works by Léger hung in Robert Mallet-Steven's entrance hall to an "Ideal French Embassy" and in Le Corbusier's Pavillon de L'Esprit Nouveau.* [1]

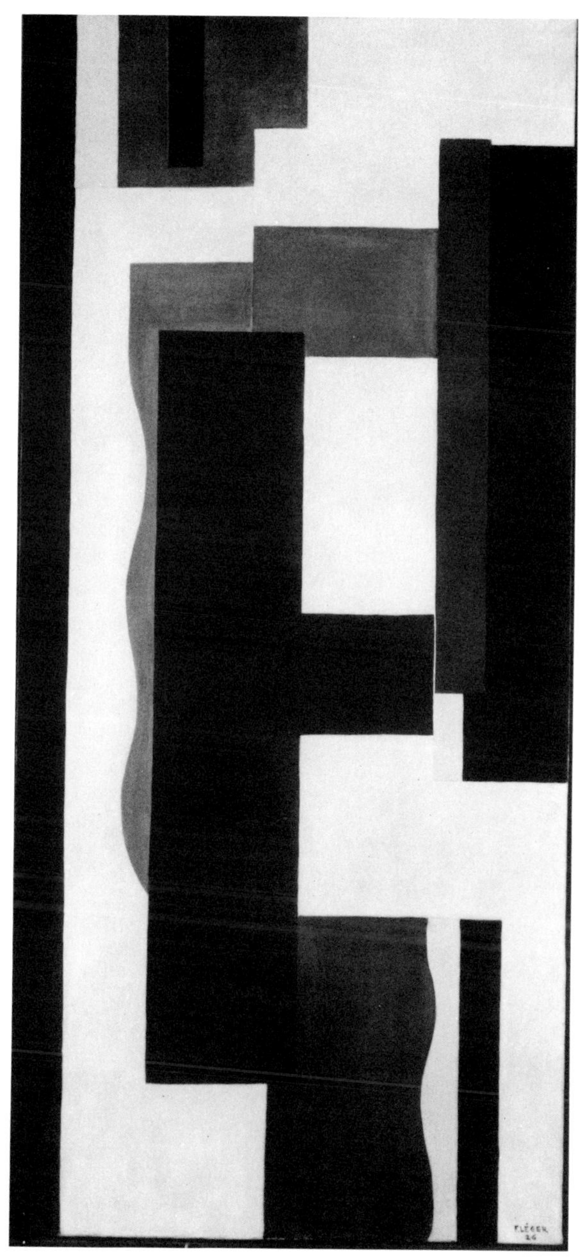

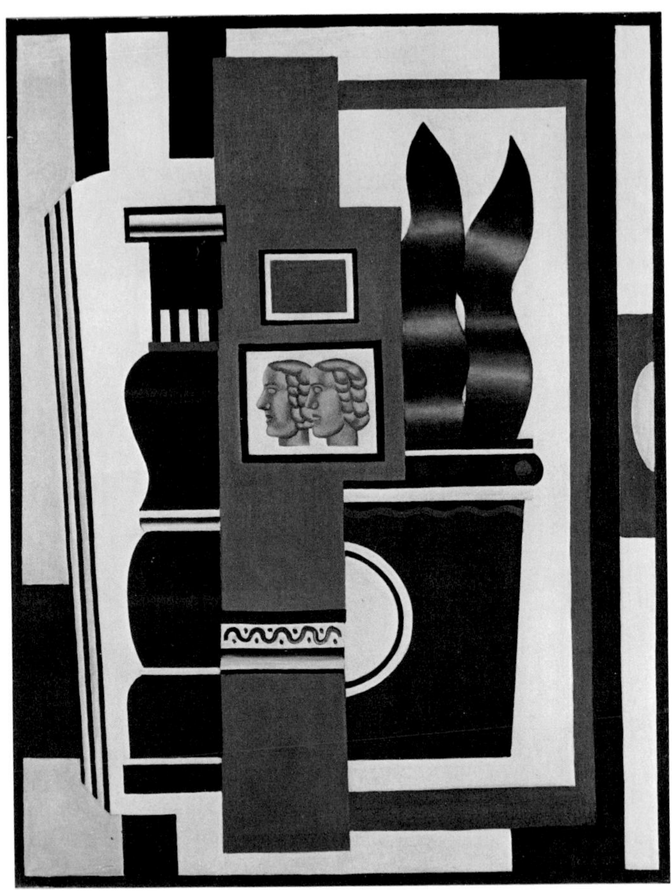

16. *Nature morte (Still Life with Cameos).* 1926. Oil on canvas. 51¼ x 38¼ (130.2 x 97.2). *F. LÉGER. 26*, lower right; *NATURE-MORTE /F. LÉGER /26,* on back.

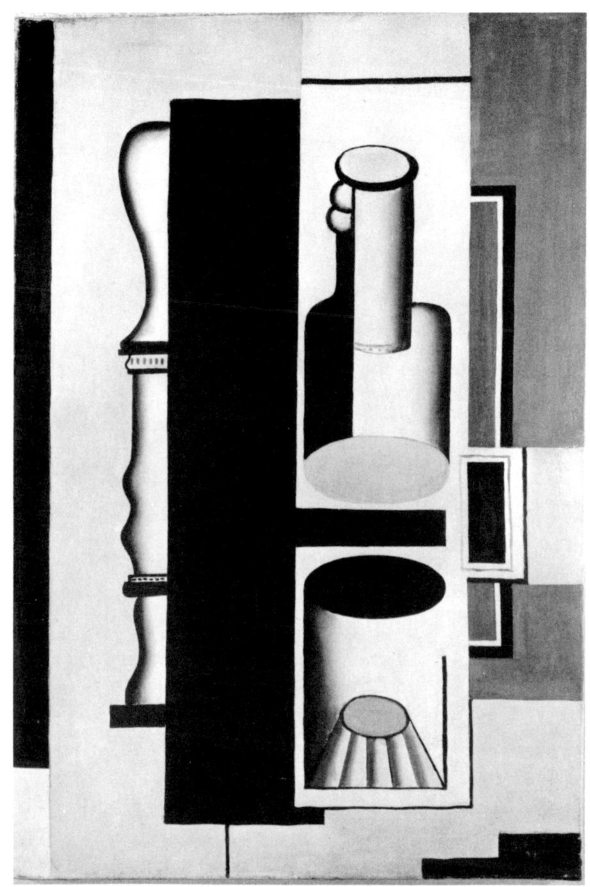

17. *Nature morte (Still Life).* 1927. Oil on canvas. 36½ x 23½ (92.7 x 59.7). *F. LÉGER/27,* lower right; *NATURE-morte/F. LEGER-27,* on back (now hidden by relining).

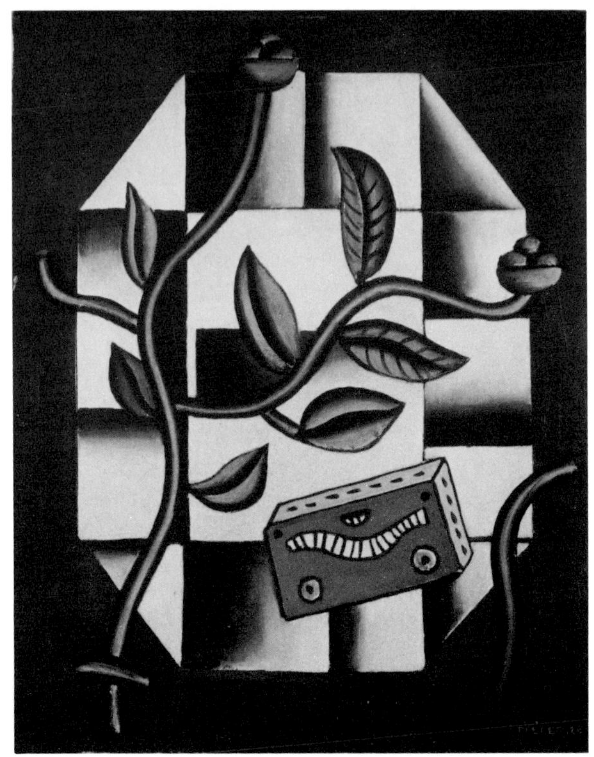

18. *Nature morte (Still Life).* 1928. Oil on canvas. 25½ x 19¾ (64.7 x 52). *F. LÉGER. 28, lower right; NATURE-MORTE/F. LEGER. 28, on back. According to Christian Zervos, this painting and cat. no. 25 were inspired by rock crystals which Léger bought at Deyrolle, the naturalist shop on the rue du Bac, Paris.*[2]

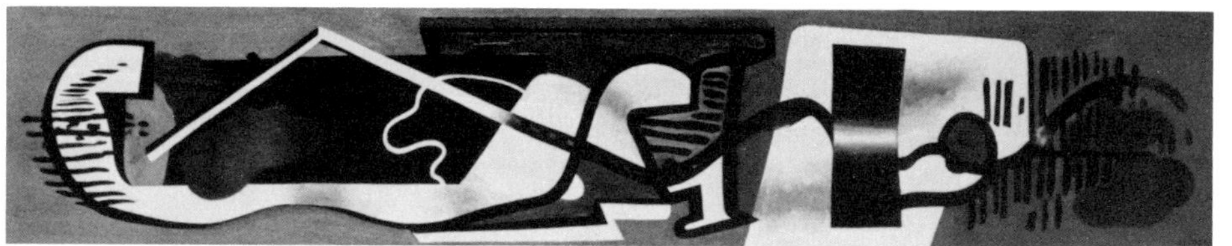

19. Winter. 1929. Oil on canvas. 13¾ x 63½ (34.9 x 161.3). *F. LEGER 29*, lower right. *This piece is one of a group of long horizontal paintings on the four seasons, all dated 1929.*[3]

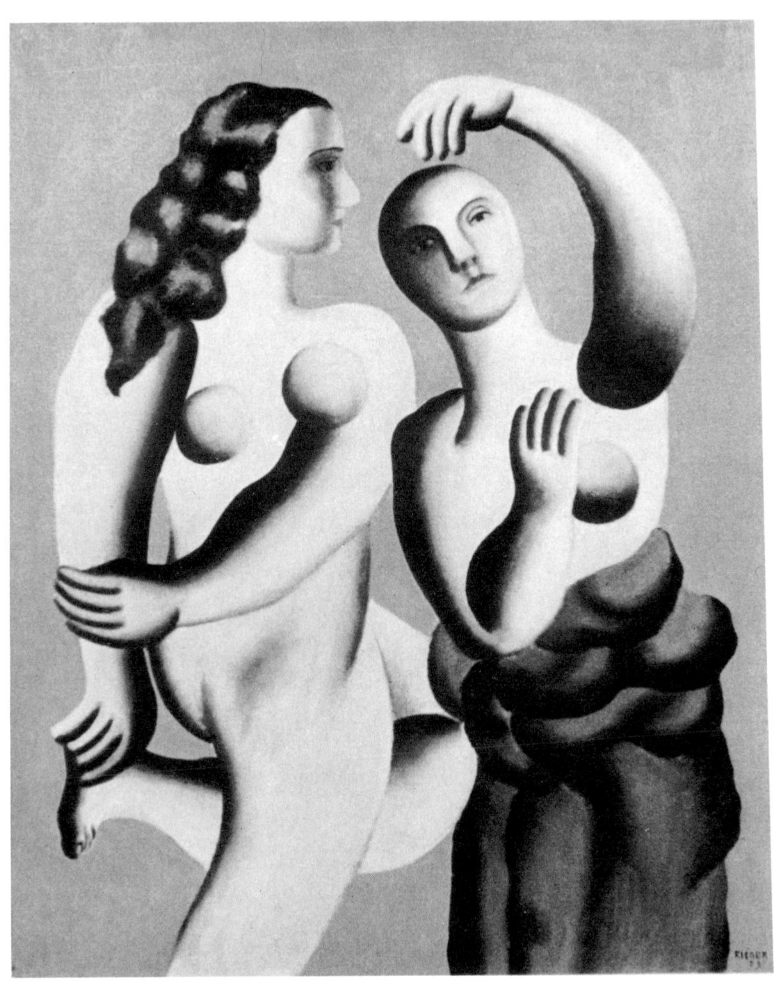

20. *Etude pour deux danseuses (Study for Two Dancers).*
1929. Oil on canvas. 36¼ x 28¾ (92.5 x 73.2). F. LEGER 29,
lower right; *ETUDE pour deux danseuses/F LEGER – 29,*
upper left, back. Collection of the Sarah Campbell Blaffer
Foundation at the University of Houston Blaffer Gallery.

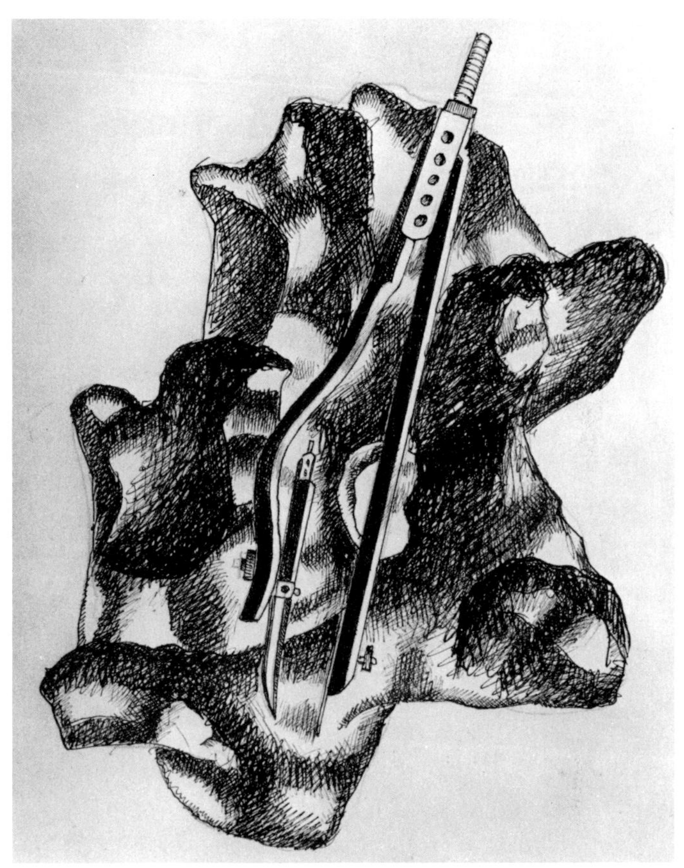

21. *Composition with Compass.* c. 1930. Pen and ink on paper. 12 x 9½ (30.5 x 24.2). Unsigned.

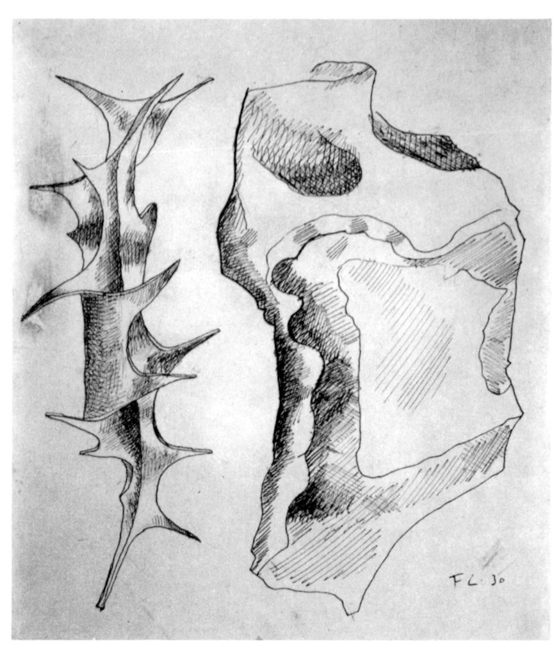

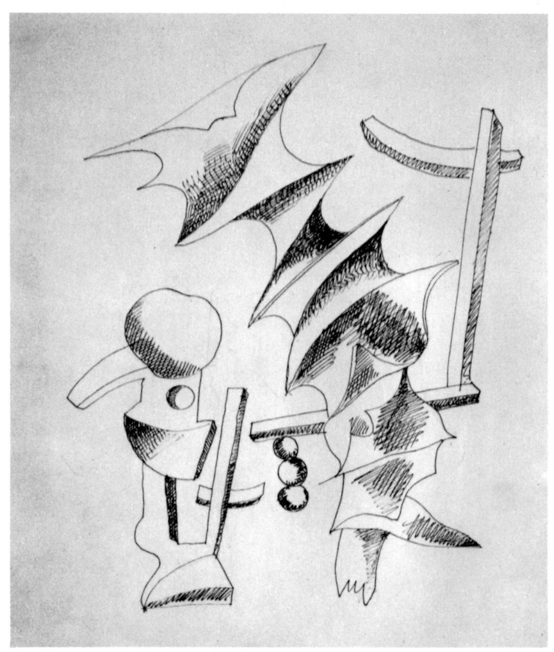

22. *Composition.* 1930. Recto-verso drawings, pen and ink on pink paper. 15⅛ x 12⅞ (38.4 x 32.7). *F L. 30, lower right recto.*

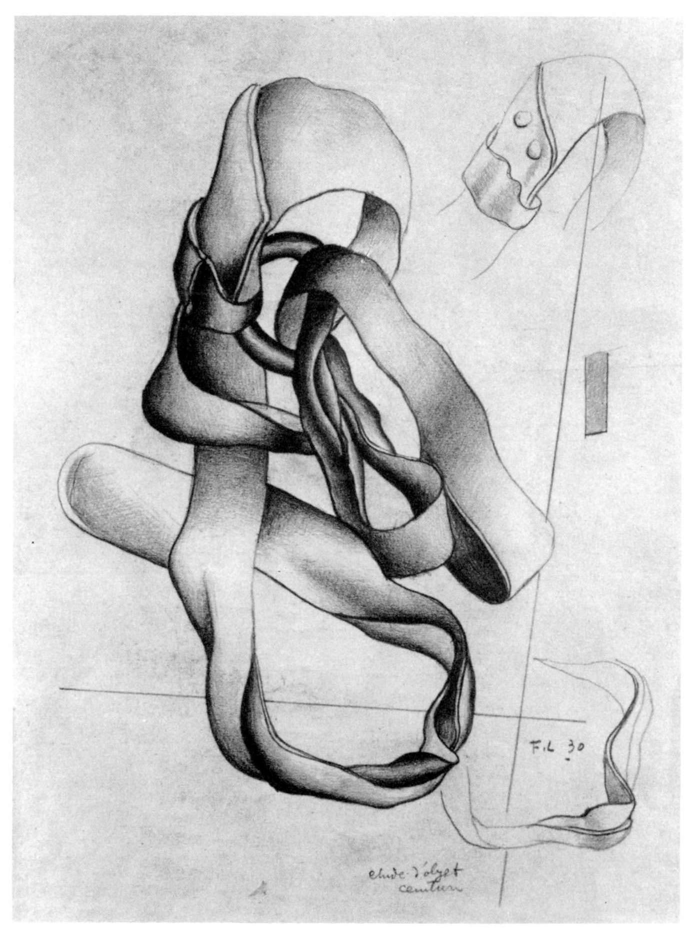

23. *Study of a Belt.* 1930. Pencil on paper. 12⅝ x 9½ (32 x 24). *F. L 30* and *etude d'objet /ceinture,* lower right.

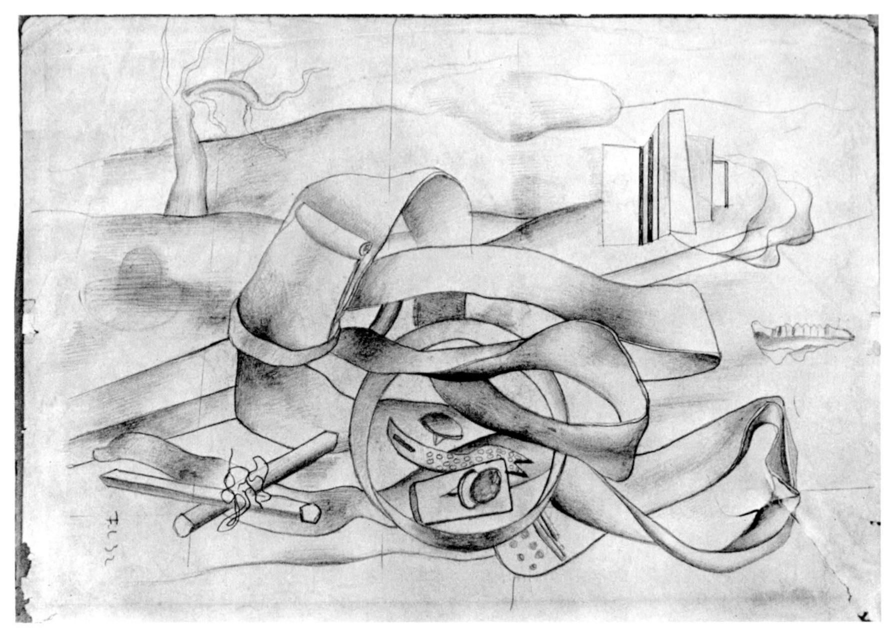

24. *Still Life with Leather Belt.* 1932. Pencil on paper. 10 x
14 (25.4 x 35.5). F. L 32, sideways, lower left.

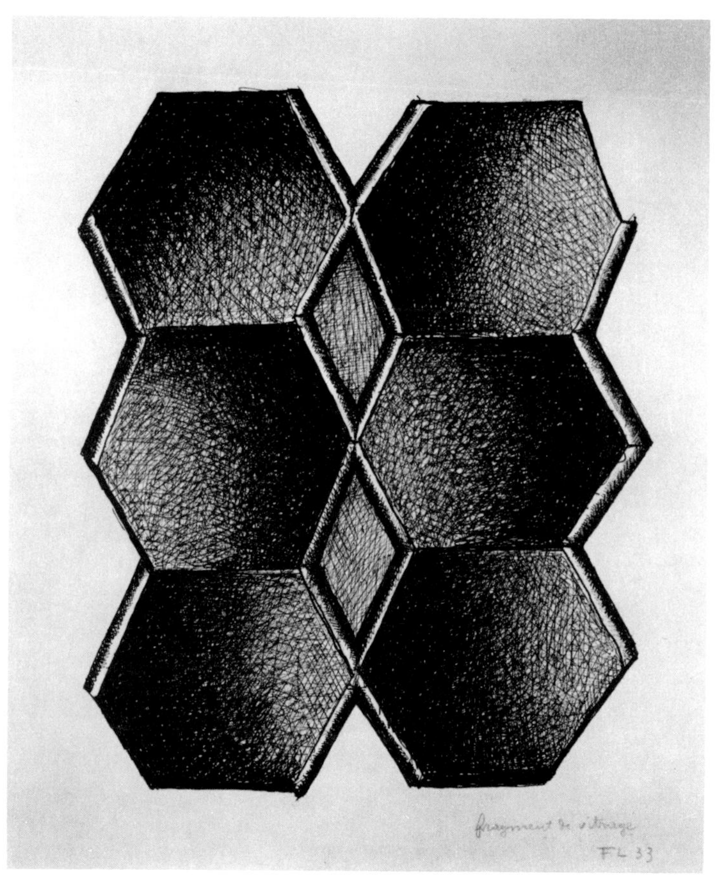

25. *Fragment de vitrage (Section of a Stained-glass Window).* 1933. Pen and ink on paper. 13½ x 11½ (34.2 x 29.2). *fragment de vitrage/F. L 33,* lower right. (See note, cat. no. 18.)

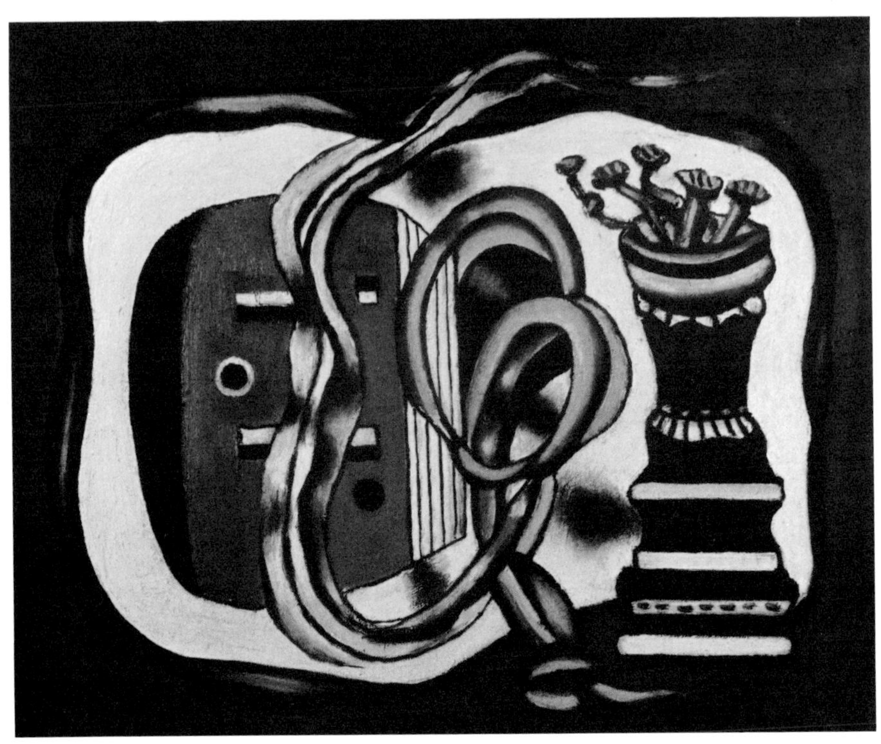

26. *Le Vase bleu (The Blue Vase).* 1936. Oil on canvas. 15 x 18 (38.1 x 45.7). F. *LÉGER*/36, lower right. Janie C. Lee Gallery, Houston.

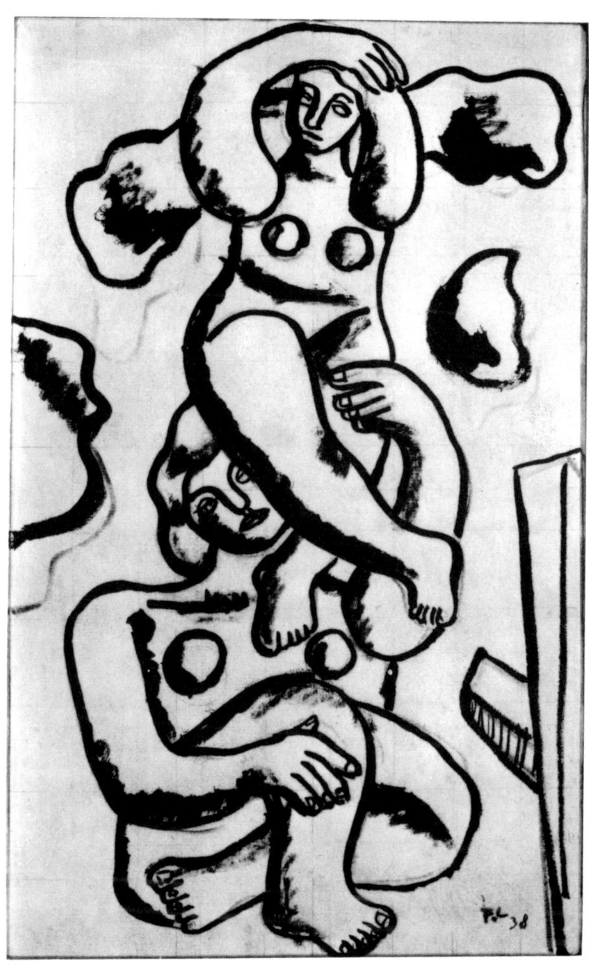

27. *Study for "Composition aux deux perroquets" (Composition with Two Parrots).* 1938. Brush and ink on paper. 15 x 9¾ (38.1 x 24.8). *F. L 38,* lower right.

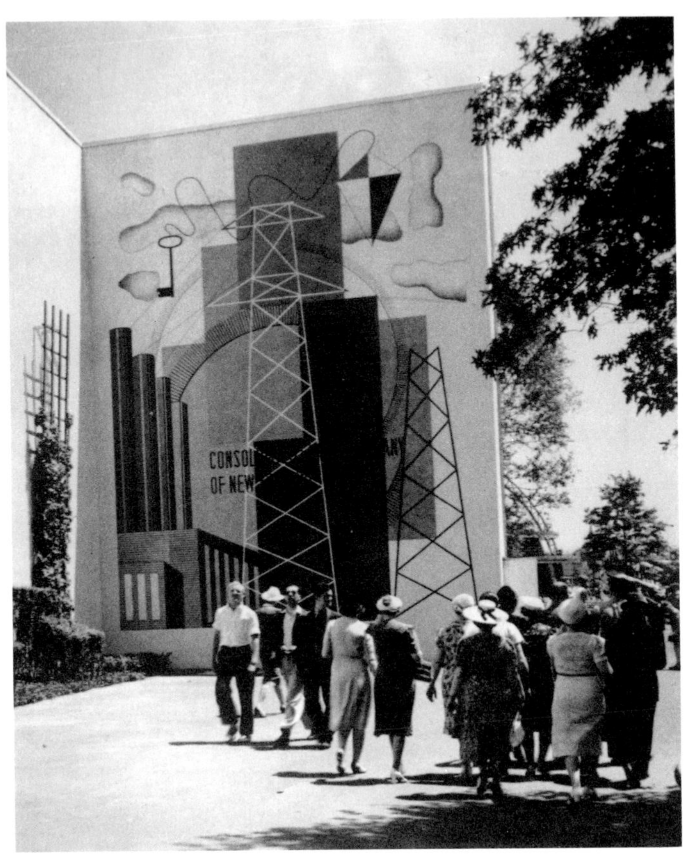

28. Three Studies for a Mural. c. 1939. (a) Watercolor on paper. 10¼ x 8¾ (26 x 22.2). (b) Pencil on paper. 10¾ x 8 (27.3 x 20.3). (c) Colored pencil on paper. 10¾ x 8½ (27.3 x 21.6). All unsigned. Mr. and Mrs. Charles V. Hooks, Houston. *Apparently, these were studies for an exterior mural on Con Edison's "City of Light" exhibit hall for the 1939 World's Fair (photo above). The mural was destroyed when the building was dismantled.*

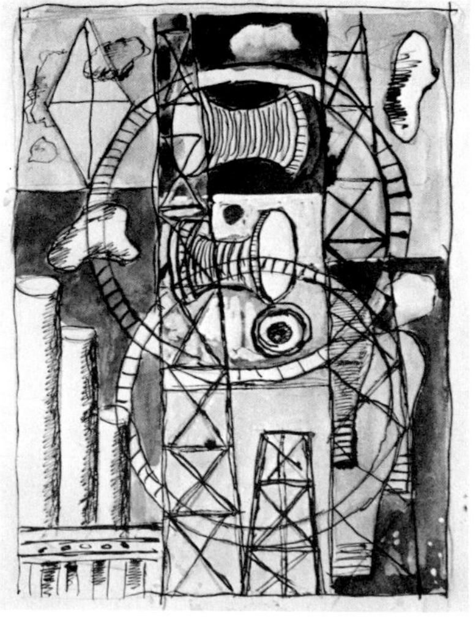

(a)

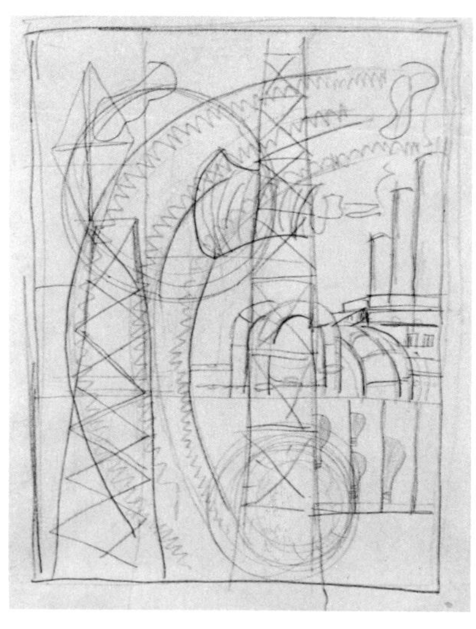

(b)

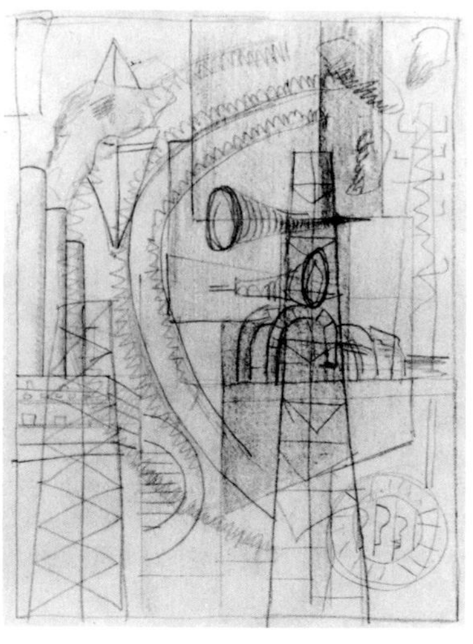

(c)

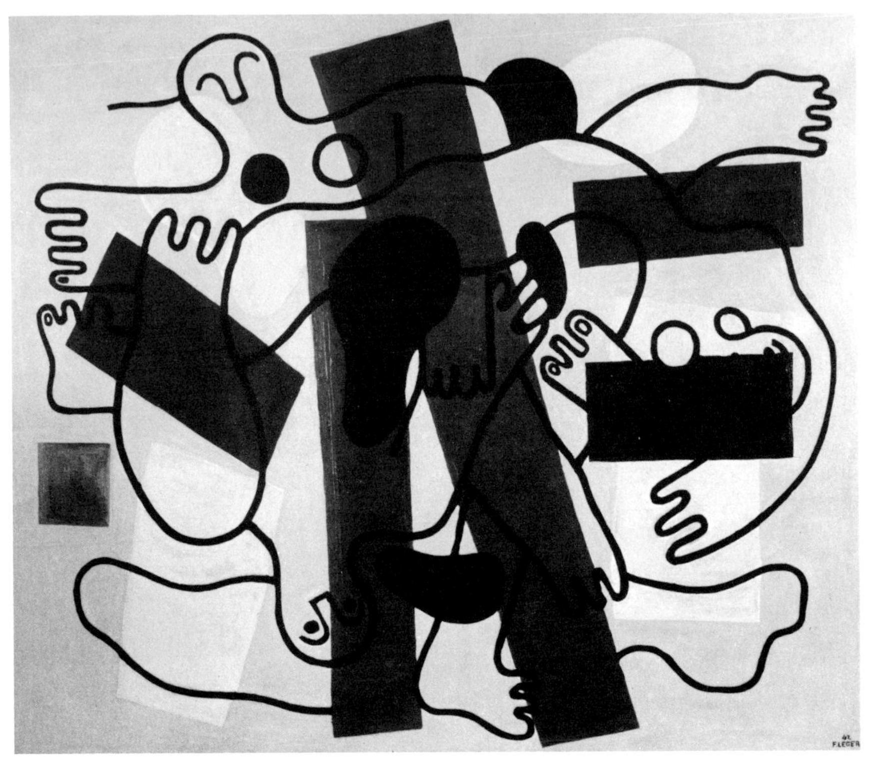

29. *Divers: Red and Black.* 1942. Oil on canvas. 50 x 58 (127 x 147.3). 42 /*F. LEGER,* lower right. Mr. and Mrs. James H. Clark, Dallas.

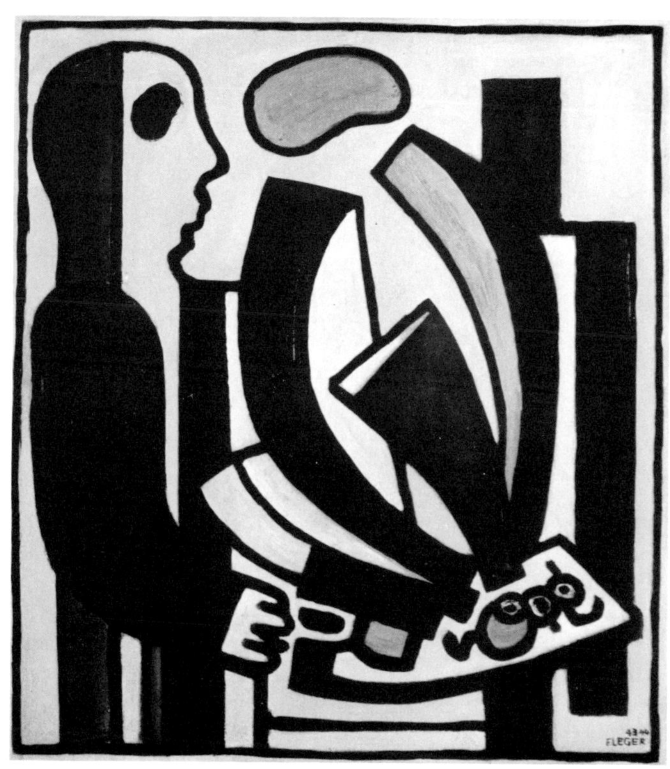

30. *Study for "L'homme au melon" (Man with Melon).*
1943-44. Oil on paper mounted on canvas. 24¾ x 22 (63 x
55.9). *43-44/F. LEGER*, lower right. Menil Foundation
Collection, Houston.

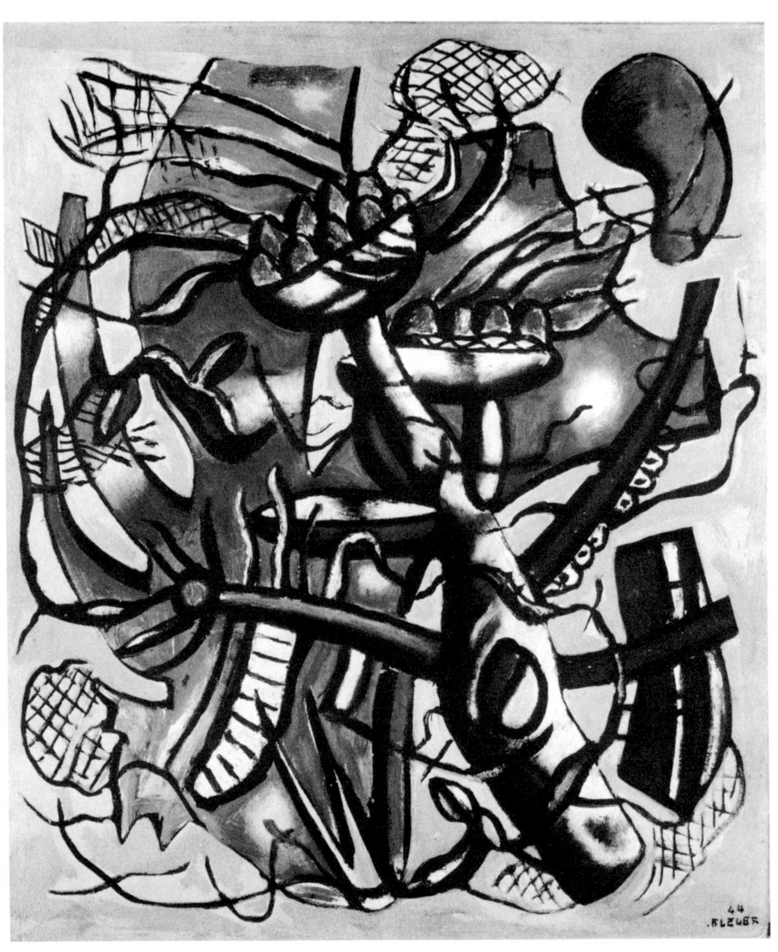

31. *Etude en violet et jaune (Study in Violet and Yellow)*.
1944. Oil on canvas mounted on board. 24 x 19⅞ (61 x 50.5).
44/.F. LEGER, lower right; *ETUDE en violet et jaune*/F
LEGER. 44, on back.

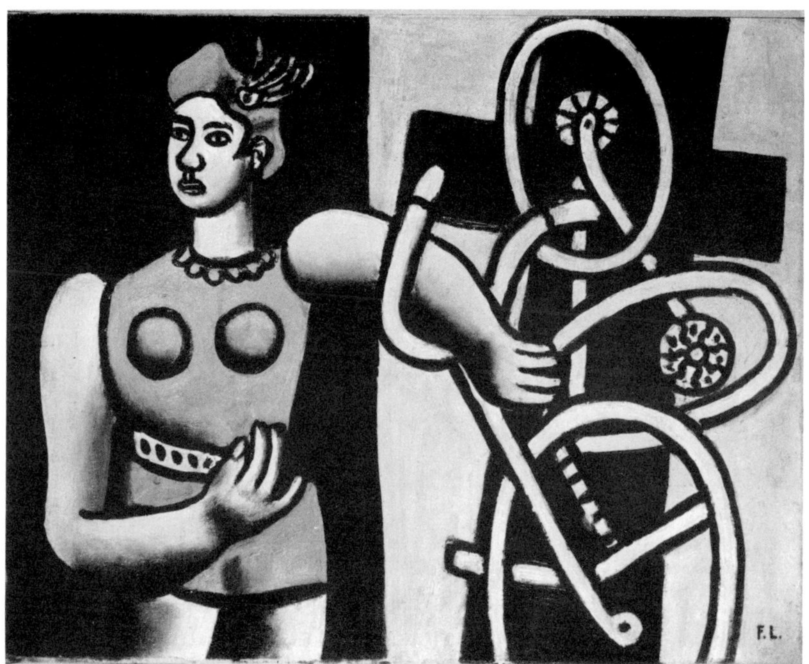

32. *Study for "La grande Julie" (Big Julie)*. 1945. Oil on
canvas. 16⅛ x 20⅛ (41 x 51.1). F.L., lower right. Menil
Foundation Collection, Houston.

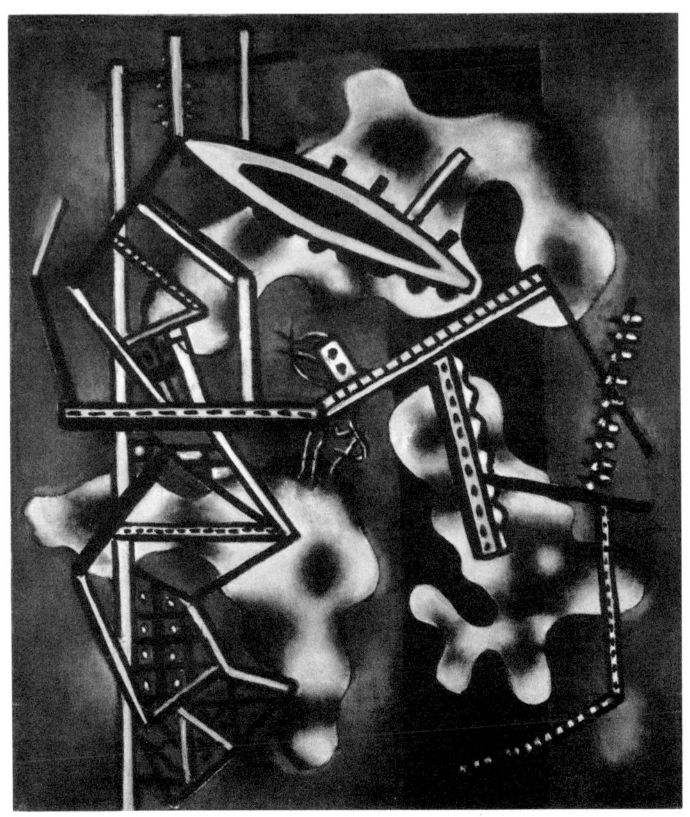

33. *Paysage, fond bleu (Landscape, Blue Background).* 1947. Oil on canvas. 25½ x 21⅜ (64.8 x 54.3). *F LEGER. 47,* lower right; *PAYSAGE 47 /F. LEGER /fond bleu,* on back.

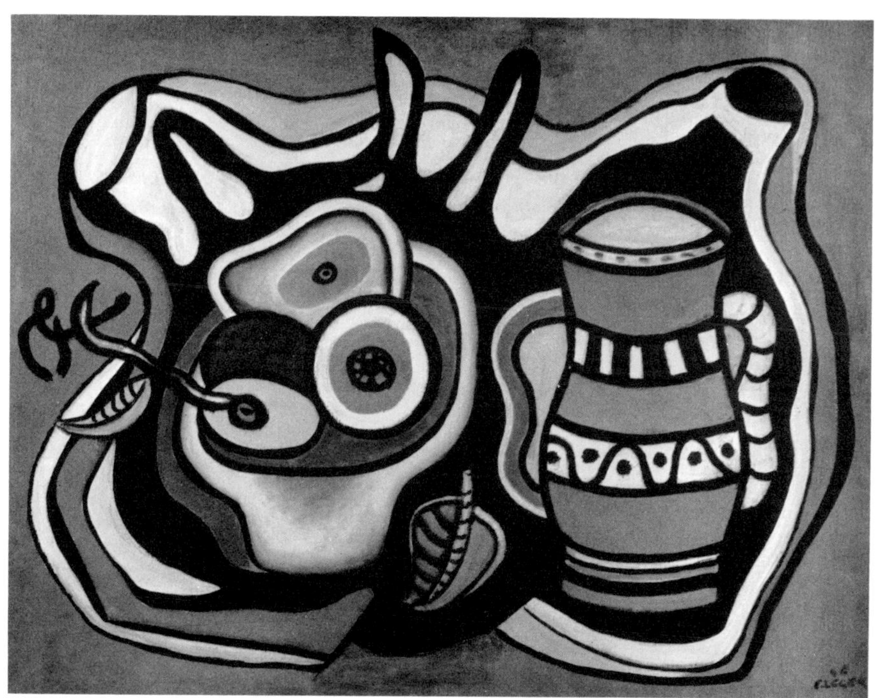

34. *Le Vase orange (The Orange Vase)*. 1946. Oil on canvas.
28¼ x 36¼ (71.8 x 92.1). 46 /*F. LEGER*, lower right; *LE VASE
ORANGE /F. LEGER /48*, on back. The Sylvan and Mary Lang
Collection, McNay Art Institute, San Antonio.

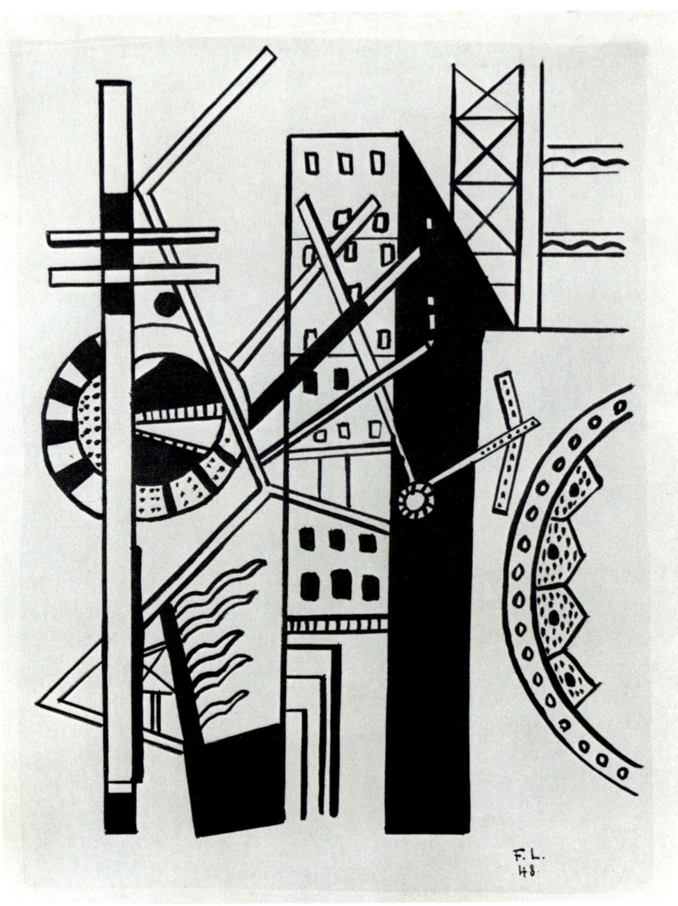

35. *Composition.* 1948. Gouache and ink on paper. 12⅞ x
9¾ (32.7 x 24.8). *F.L.* /48, lower right.

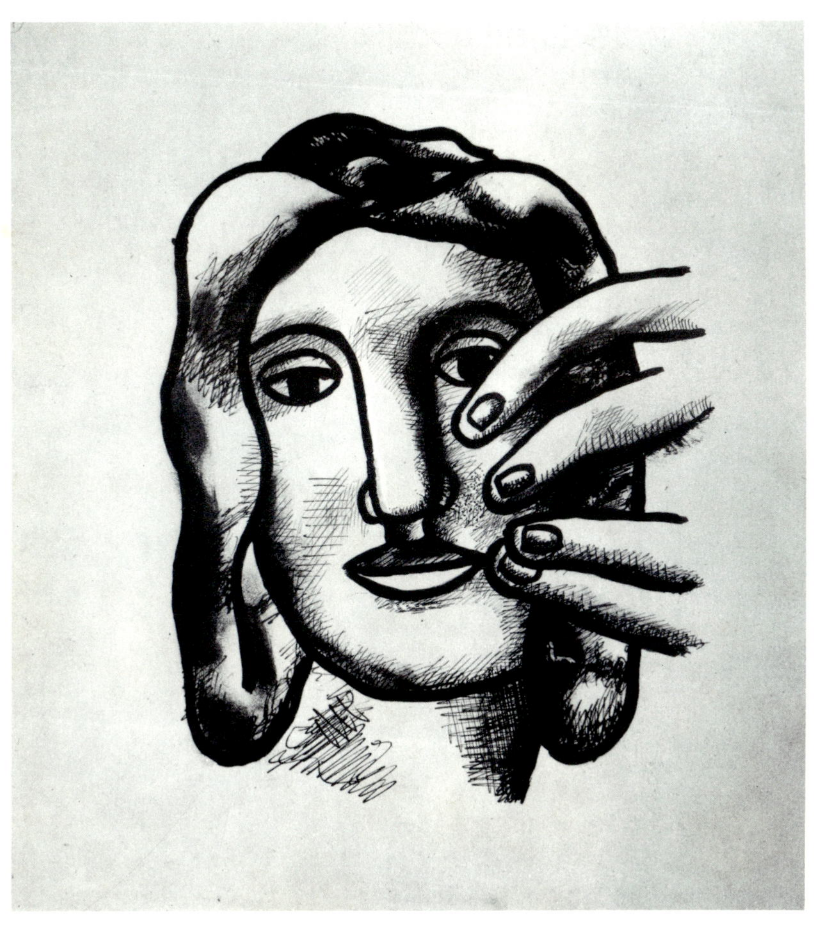

36. *Tête de femme (Head of a Woman)*. 1948. Brush, pen,
and ink on paper. 12 x 10½ (30.5 x 26.7). Unsigned.

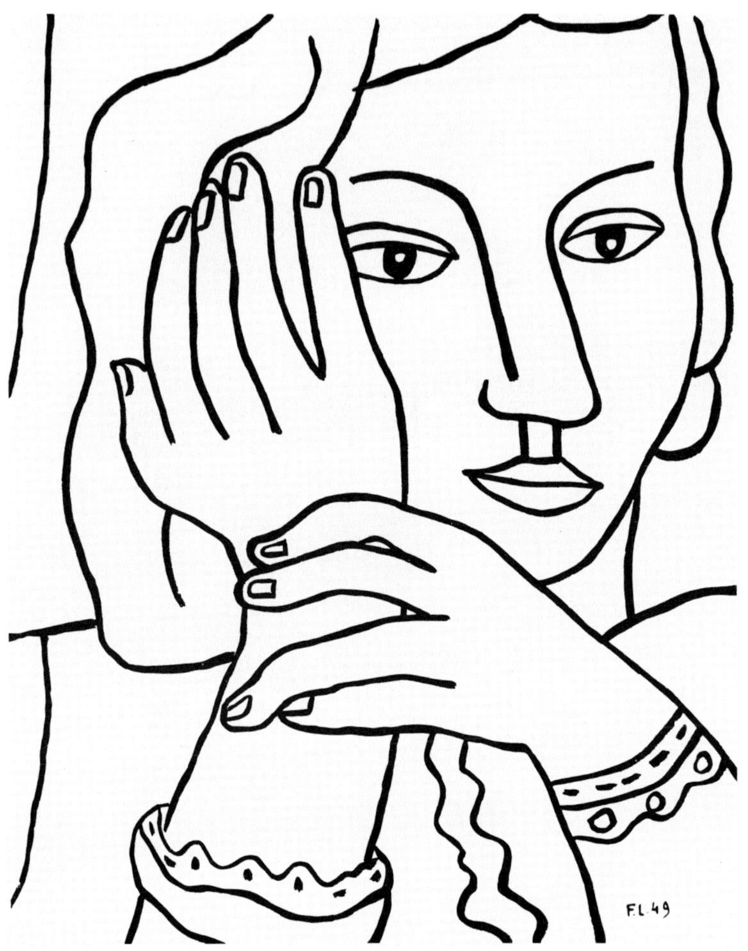
37. *Etude pour "La Partie de campagne" (Study for "The Country Outing").* 1949. Brush and ink on paper. 25¾ x 19¾ (65.4 x 50.2). *F.L. 49,* lower right.

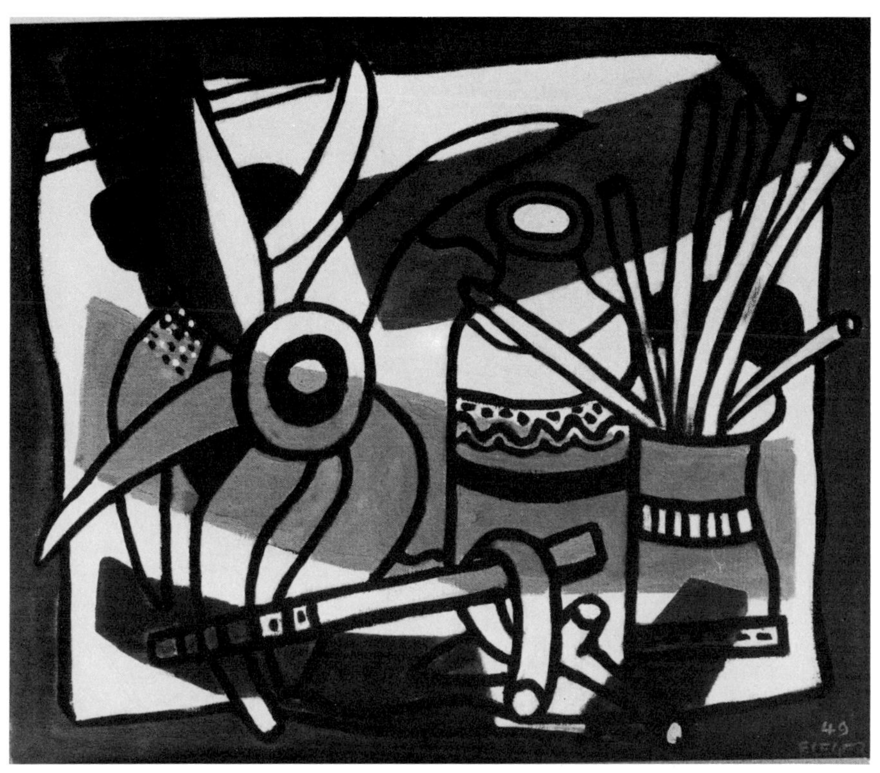

38. *Un Vase et une fleur (Vase and Flower).* 1949. Oil on canvas. 21¼ x 25½ (54 x 64.8). 49 /F. LEGER, lower right; *UN VASE et une Fleur/F LEGER/49*, on back.

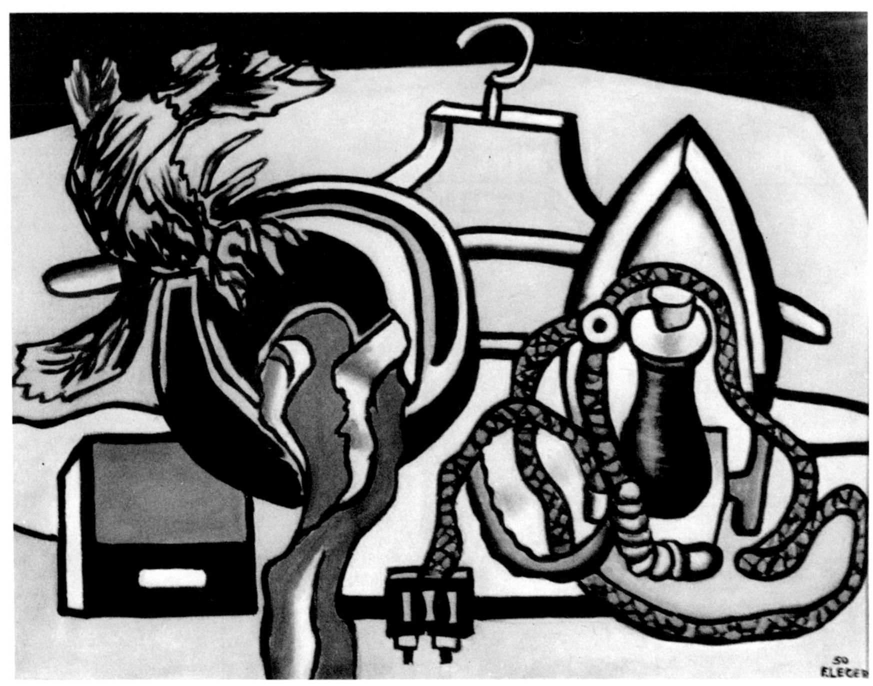

39. *Le Chapeau vert et le fer à répasser (Green Hat and Iron).* 1950. Oil on canvas. 28¾ x 36¼ (73 x 92.1). *50/F. LEGER,* lower right; *le chapeau VERT et le fer a répasser/F. LEGER. 50,* on back. Jeffrey Horvitz Ltd., Los Angeles.

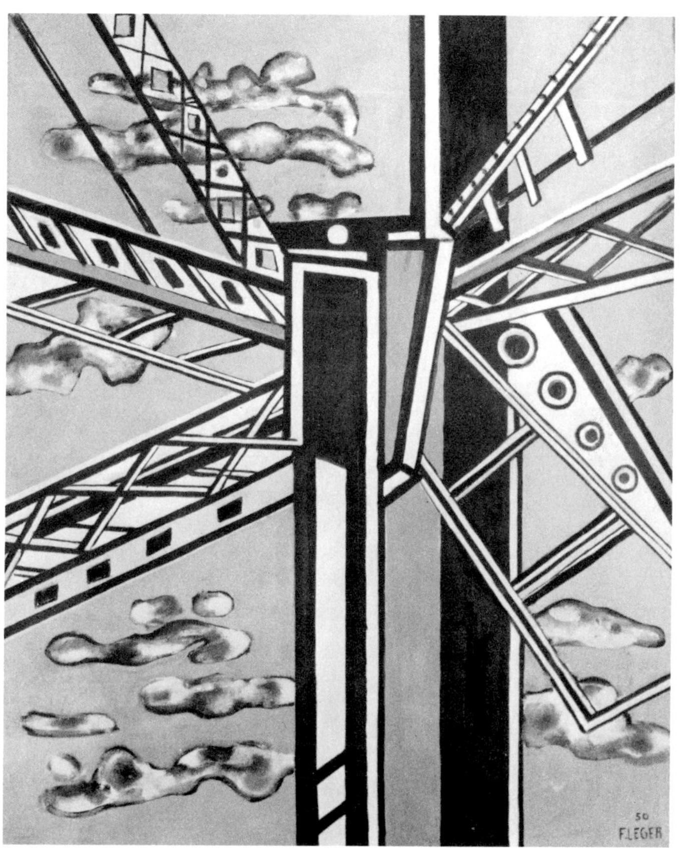

40. *Elément mécanique sur fond jaune (Structural Element on Yellow Background).* 1950. Oil on canvas. 36⅛ x 28¾ (91.7 x 73). *50/F. LEGER*, lower right; *ELEMENT/MECANIQUE/SUR FOND JAUNE/F. LEGER. 50*, on back.

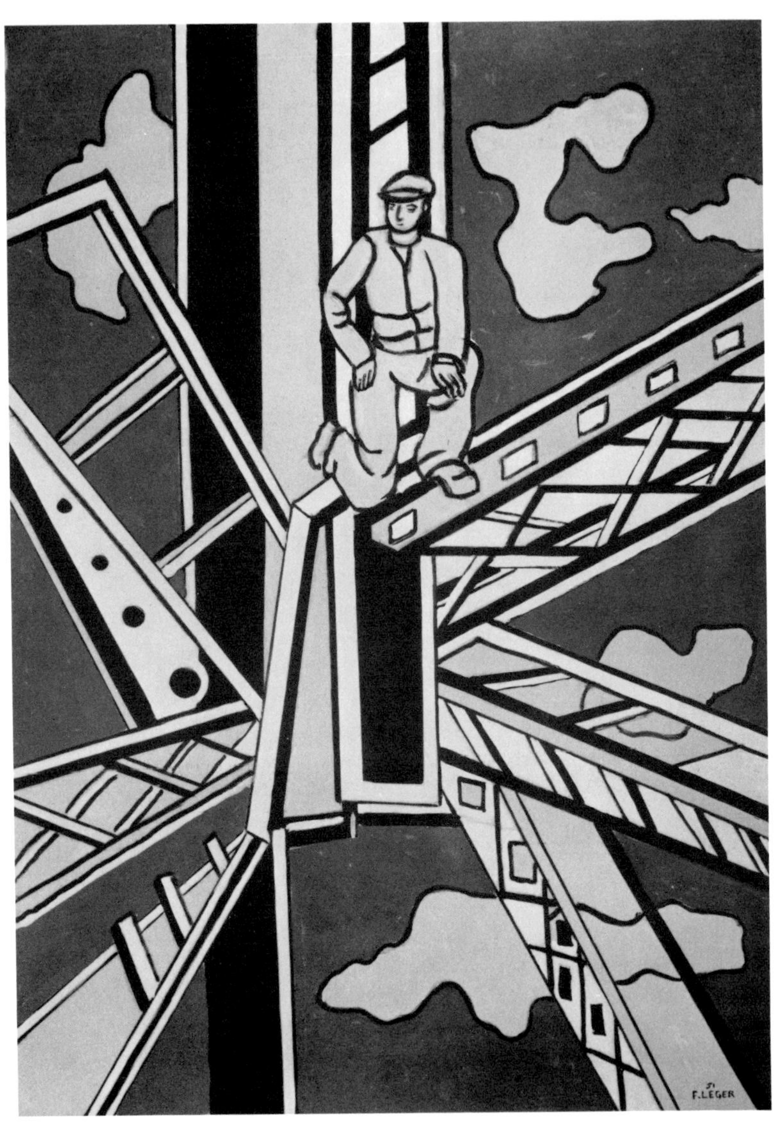

41. *Study on Red Ground for "Les Constructeurs" (The Builders).* 1951. Oil on canvas. 51 x 34¾ (129.5 x 88.3). 51/F. LEGER, lower right; LES/CONSTRUCTEU/RS/F. LEGER/51, on back. Menil Foundation Collection, Houston.

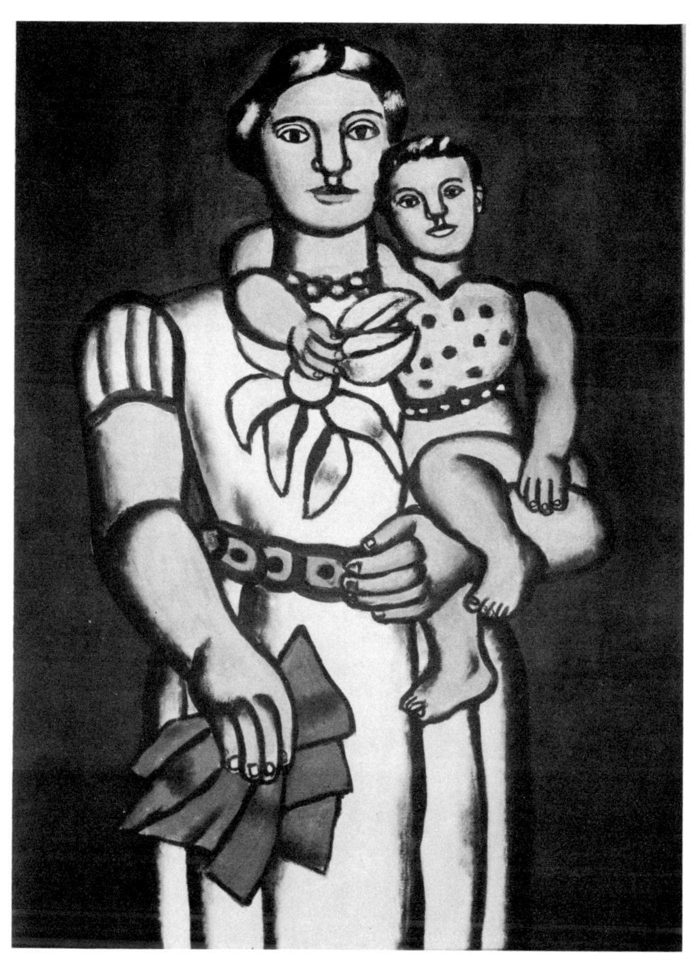

42. *La Mère et l'enfant (Mother and Child).* 1951. Oil on canvas. 36¼ x 25¾ (92.1 x 65.4). 51/*F. LEGER,* lower right; *LA MÈRE et l'enfant/F. LEGER.* 51, on back.

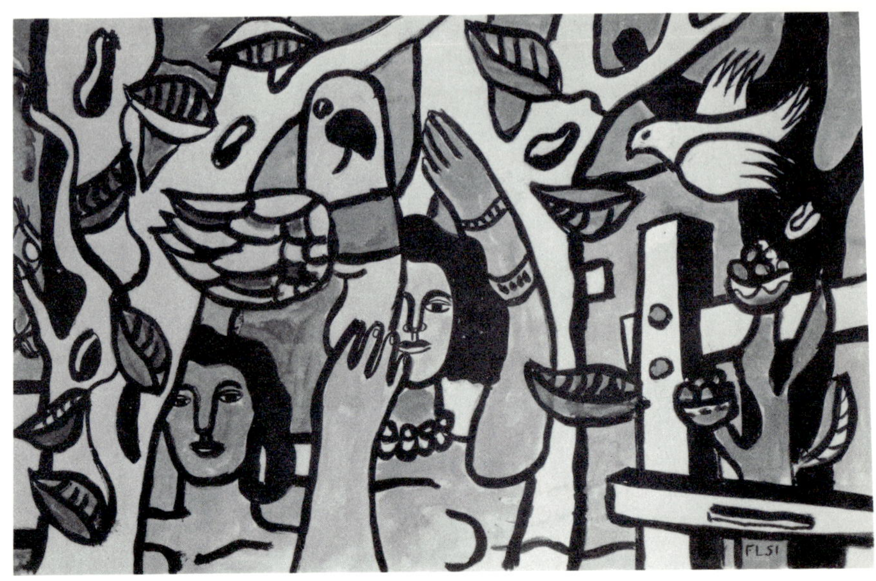

43. *Composition with Women and Birds.* 1951. Gouache
and ink on cardboard. 15½ x 23¾ (39.3 x 60.3). F L 51,
lower right.

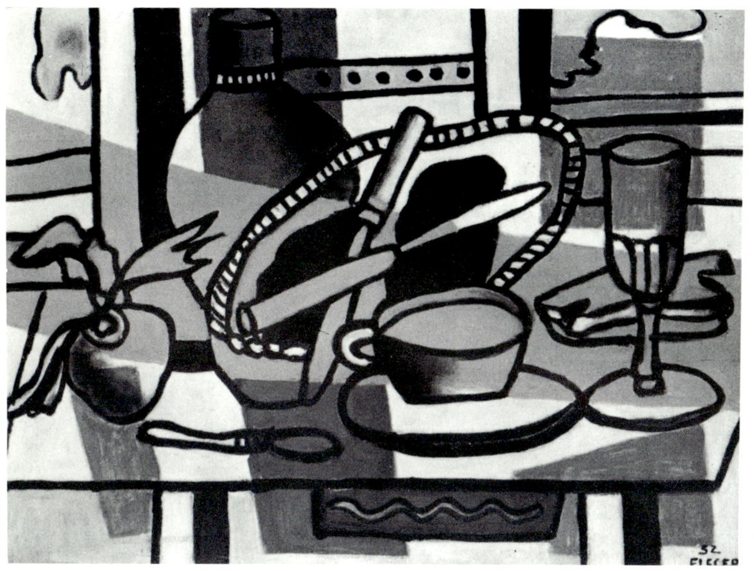

44. *Nature morte aux deux couteaux (Still Life with Two Knives).* 1952. Oil on canvas. 19¾ x 25⅝ (50 x 65). 52/F. LEGER, lower right; *Nature Morte aux deux Couteaux F Leger 52,* on back. Lois and George de Menil, Paris.

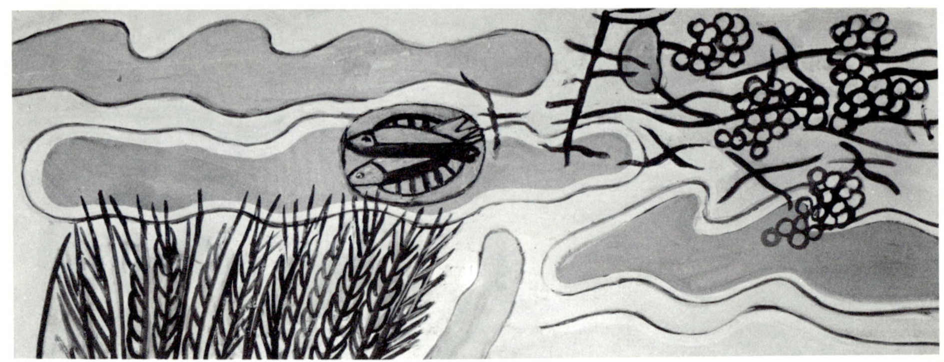

45. *Study for the Audincourt Tapestry.* c. 1953. Gouache on paper. 9⅞ x 25⅜ (25.3 x 64.4). *à Madame et Monsieur de Menil/Premiere ébauche de/la Tapisserie de Fernand Leger/pour l'eglise d'Audincourt/En temoignage de reconnaissance/L Prenel/cure,* inscribed in ink, verso. Menil Foundation Collection, Houston.

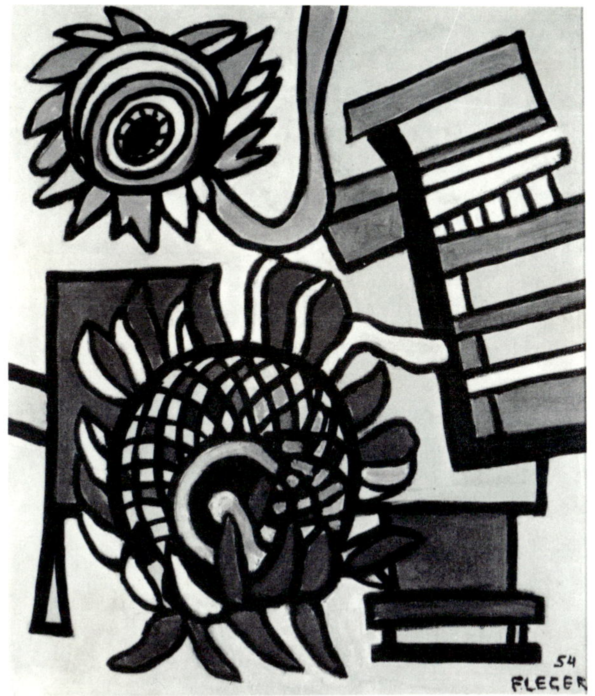

46. *Deux Tournesols (Two Sunflowers).* 1954. Oil on canvas.
18 x 14⅞ (45.7 x 37.8). 54/F. LEGER, lower right; *deux
tournesols fond bleu et jaune F. Léger 54* and *A Yvonne,* on
back. Lois and George de Menil, Paris.

1. See Christopher Green, *Léger and the Avant-Garde* (New Haven
   and London, Yale University Press, 1976), pp. 286-309 and
   Angelica Zander Rudenstine, *The Guggenheim Museum Collection: Paintings 1880-1945* (New York, Solomon R. Guggenheim
   Foundation, 1976), vol. II, pp. 469-73.

2. University of St. Thomas, Houston, *Look Back: An Exhibition of
   Cubist Paintings and Sculptures from the Menil Family Collection* (1968), p. 50.

3. G. di San Lazzaro, editor, *Homage to Fernand Léger* (New York,
   Tudor Publishing Co.), p. 45.